# Love, Limits, & Lessons®
## A Parent's Guide to Raising Cooperative Kids

## Bill Corbett

Cooperative Kids

D1362351

Praise for
# Love, Limits, & Lessons®

"This is a must-read for every parent who has the courage to take the road less traveled in raising cooperative, drug-free, and bully-proof kids. This practical and inspiring instruction manual offers parents invaluable tips & tools for doing the most important work they'll ever do."

- **Diana Loomans**, author, *What All Children Want Their Parents to Know; Twelve Keys to Raising a Happy Child*

"Bill Corbett has many years of experience as a parent, grandparent, and stepparent and brings this to his professional life as a parent educator with great skill. His practical advice, based on common sense, warm humor, and love for children shines through in his work."

- **Barbara Nicholson**, M.Ed., Co-Founder, President of the Board of Directors Attachment Parenting International

"If your child has ever exasperated you and left you in a quandary about how to parent, help is here. From tackling tantrums, dealing with bullies, and setting boundaries, *Love, Limits, & Lessons®* is full of sound wisdom for raising a family."

- **Grace Durfee**, Professional Certified Coach, author of *Balance with Grace: Celebrate the Kaleidoscope of Life*, www.balancewithgrace.com.

"In this book, Corbett helps parents to compassionately meet the needs of their children by understanding their motivations. This easy to read guide provides practical methods and personal examples leading to appropriate limits and knowledgeable and loving guidance. *Loves, Limits & Lessons®* will lead to young brains developing and thriving in environments filled with love and structure."

- **Deborah McNelis**, M.S., author of, The Brain Development Series, owner/creator of braininsights®

"One thing is acutely evident — Bill Corbett cares. He cares that we are successful at parenting so that we raise happy, secure, independent children capable of great contribution. However, as a parent, I understand that the future is now and this is why his book is so important. Bill gives us practical, step by step, methods to deal with the immediacy of decision making and behavior in the "trenches". As you read his book, something very interesting happens — you not only discover how to become a better parent, but you begin looking into yourself, and find how you can become a better person. "

- **Charles F. Glassman**, MD, FACP; author of *Brain Drain – The Breakthrough That Will Change Your Life*; Founder of The New York Center for Longevity & Wellness and Coach MD, LLC.

"Becoming familiar with Bill Corbett's work has had a profound effect on my ability to guide my children and to teach them positive communication and conflict resolution skills. His techniques are magical and easy to apply. "

- **T. DeFriest**, parent; mom to Olivia and Natalie

"*Loves, Limits & Lessons®* has evolved from one man's passion to help parents, grandparents and caregivers of those precious ones small in stature but close to our hearts: our children. Bill Corbett has taken his own painful beginnings and written a clear, concise and easy to read manual for those of us struggling to be better parents. Don't wait until your kids go off to college to learn how to get their needs met, solve their own problems and get along with others. There is no drive thru on the way home that will sell us better parenting skills. Every life has moments that change us forever and make us who we are. I feel so fortunate to have met Bill at a time in my life when I needed to know what to do with my own power-struggling grandchild. *Loves, Limits & Lessons®* was written with the pen of experience by a man who has truly found his purpose in life."

- **Susan Sherrill**, Licensed Occupational Therapist, grandparent to Jackson, Brenden, Nathan, Kyla, and Reagan

"Bill's techniques have helped me create firm boundaries and avoid frustrating power struggles at home. Now I have more tools to raise my son in a positive and encouraging household!"

- **Kellie Paluck**, mother of Dillon

"*Love, Limits, & Lessons®* offers a clear, manageable guide for anyone who interacts with children. As a parent, teacher, and school administrator, I consider this a tremendously valuable resource!"

- **K. Meagan Ledendecker**, Educational Administrator

"Children don't come with a manual but if they did, it would be *Love, Limits & Lessons®* by Bill Corbett. Each chapter is a quick, yet powerful read and the font style and size makes it inviting to keep reading, page after page. Constructed in a directory style rather than a cover-to-cover read, Bill's book allows parents to select the issue they are dealing with and go right to that chapter to get the advice they need. The best part of this book is that a parent of a young child can find the information he or she needs, then consult it again a few years later when the age of the children and the challenges change. This is a must read for every parent who hopes to raise cooperative kids."

- **Neil Haley**, Radio Talk Show Host, CEO of Total Tutor.

"It often appears that parents work on their health, careers and businesses but assume that good parenting happens automatically. Thank you Bill for this amazing blueprint for raising successful children. I trust parents everywhere will learn to "release the music" in their children and be pleased with the sound produced."

- **Dan Miller**, author *48 Days to the Work You Love.*

"Education of our children has changed drastically over the past 20 years. Parents are looking to educators for help and educators are looking to parents for support. Thank you Bill for providing guidance for both groups! *Love, Limits & Lessons®* is a must read for any classroom teacher!"

- **Janine A. Preston**, MA/NYU; classroom educator K-12; adjunct professor/NYU; parent

**Cooperative Kids**

# Love, Limits & Lessons®
## A Parent's Guide to Raising Cooperative Kids

**Bill Corbett**

Love, Limits, & Lessons®
© 2012 by Bill Corbett
All rights reserved.

Cover designed by T. Lak
Cover illustrated by Rick Lamarre

Cooperative Kids Publishing
www.CooperativeKids.com

ISBN-13: 978-0-9821121-3-7
ISBN-10: 0-9821121-3-0

*Printed in the United States of America.*

No part of this book may be reprinted, reproduced or utilized in whole or in part in any form without written permission except in the case of brief quotations embodied in critical articles or reviews.

# Dedication

To my mother Bernadine, whose loving spirit protected us as children when evil fell upon our home. You're a survivor and have passed on your strength and courage to each of us. Your warm encouragement continues to guide me so that I am able to fulfill my dreams.

To my children Aubrey, Shauna, and Billy, who helped me learn how to become the father I never had. Each of you survived my trial and error attempts at parenting until I got it right. Thank you for letting me drag you along on all the early days of my seminars and workshops to run video cameras, registration tables, and book sales. Most of all, thank you for enduring the embarrassment as I told and retold the stories of how my methods worked.

To my stepdaughter Olivia who became my unsuspecting target of lifestyle changes that included family meetings, house rules, and other boundaries. What a joy it has been to have had the chance to be a dad all over again and for the privilege of giving you piggyback rides through the house. I'm honored to have tucked you in at night and watched you grow.

To my loving wife Elizabeth who has given me everything that I had only dreamed of having in a partner and a friend. You have believed in me from the very beginning, especially on all those late evenings spent alone or sitting next to my empty place setting at the dinner table, while I was studying for psychology exams or writing this book. God has truly blessed me with the chance to love and be loved as He intended marriage to be.

# CONTENTS

# Musings and Acknowledgments

Oh no, there's something wrong with my preschooler! She's going to get thrown out of her daycare! No other school will take her and I'll be forced to quit my job! I'll be visiting her in juvenile hall as a teenager someday! Or worse yet, she'll be 30 and still living with me for the rest of my life! These were just some of the fears that may have been running through my mind as I drove home with my almost 4-year-old daughter Aubrey after picking her up from daycare late one afternoon in 1983.

Earlier that day, school officials had called me at my office to tell me that they were having some problems with Aubrey and the director needed to speak to me when I arrived to pick her up after work. At the meeting, the director and my daughter's teacher revealed to me that Aubrey was demonstrating what they termed advanced supervisory skills and, as a result, was disrupting classrooms. They went on to describe how she would randomly get up from an activity in her class, take one or two other children with her, and then walk to another play group. There, she would hand-pick a few more children and lead them all to another activity of her choosing, such as coloring on an easel, playing with a special set of blocks or looking at picture books. The amazing thing was that the children would follow her and comply.

But the problems didn't stop there. Not only was she redirecting the classroom activities, but she was also constantly spinning tales and telling the other children things the staff felt she shouldn't. During playtime she would gather any children who would listen and tell them elaborate stories. The director warned me that her behavior was becoming difficult to manage and I may need to consider finding another daycare if her cooperation didn't improve.

On the ride home, I struggled to determine how to fix this problem. As a young father, what discipline was I supposed to come up with for behavior that appeared to be early stages of leadership and storytelling skills at age 3? My deep thoughts were disrupted when my daughter suddenly declared, "Daddy, when my legs get a little bit longer, I'm going to have a baby." In a sudden state of shock, I nearly drove off the road and quickly turned to look at her. I exclaimed, "What!?" She then went on to tell me where babies come from, starting with a process of growing in trees. When the baby sees a lady she wants as her mother, she jumps down from the tree and runs up behind the lady. According to her story, the baby then grabs onto the lady's ankle, climbs up her leg, and magically goes into her body. She then said, "And when it's time to be born, they come out of her body and say 'Hi Mommy, I'm here!'" I forced a smile and turned my attention back to the road ahead. I thought to myself, if this is what she's coming up with at 3, I am frightened to think about what the teen years would bring. I later learned that her teacher became pregnant, was absent for a few weeks to have her baby, and then returned to school. My daughter watched the teacher's belly grow and then saw her reappear after an absence weeks later with no belly and a new baby. She filled in the missing details with her own creative imagination. I then spent the next 12 years learning everything I could about being an effective parent, and Aubrey tested me all along the way. She continued to challenge me with her curiosity, exploration and intense creativity, right into her teen years. When I looked for help, the only books on parenting back then were written by psychologists and pediatricians and were difficult to read and arduous to comprehend. Parenting classes were nonexistent.

My own father had a distorted view of parenting. When combined with his boxing career, drug and alcohol abuse, the resulting domestic violence created a poor model of parenting that I knew was wrong. Possibly more of a blessing in disguise, it taught me what family life shouldn't be like. His abusive parenting actually started me on a journey that led to writing this book and my other work in the field of parenting and discipline. In a strange sort of way, I may have him to thank for some of my success.

I also have my children to thank for what they taught me. My second little princess was born in 1985 and taught me so much about love. She also taught me how important it was to be consciously aware of what I was teaching through my parenting. While her older sister was more internally focused on the amazing and adventurous world of her creative mind, Shauna's loving and sensitive nature helped me better understand how to be a more encouraging father and to praise less often. She would interact with me for the sole purpose of gaining my attention, and believed wholeheartedly in what I told her. This sensitivity taught me to be careful about how I reacted and spoke to her. Just before our first trip to Disney World in Florida one year, Shauna contracted chicken pox. Afraid she would scratch her blisters and not allow them to heal in time for us to leave on our trip, I did a dumb dad thing. I told her that the disease was called chicken pox because if you scratched them, you would turn into a chicken. It worked. She became frightened that she could possibly grow feathers and refrained from scratching to avoid the transformation. Many years later in her tween years she became very angry with me when she learned that Santa Claus was a myth. She's still mad at me on this one. My third teacher, my son, arrived on the planet in 1987, and from him I learned the importance of parental integrity. Billy had a remarkable way of keeping track of every incident in which I may not have handled my frustration or anger very well, and reminding me for years of each moment. My little buddy helped me examine my parenting skills by questioning and challenging me every step of the way, teaching me how to build the skills I needed to raise responsible, self-assured and cooperative children.

One hot summer day while on a family vacation, we were sitting down to a picnic-style lunch at a park. Billy was about 5 or 6. Without warning, a tremendous thunderstorm came over a nearby mountain and it began to pour. The kids ran to our minivan rental for cover while we frantically packed everything up in hopes of saving the food. After just a few moments in the hot van, the kids began to fight and argue. Out of the corner of my eye I could see the minivan rocking back and forth from the ruckus inside. Becoming aware of this, feeling cold and wet from the rain, and angry that our picnic was ruined, I felt myself losing my cool and headed for the van. I remember that my intention was just to stop the fighting. I had no control over the weather or my discomfort in my wet clothes, and I couldn't do anything about the food and supplies that were now spoiled from the rain. The only thing I could try to control was the noise from the van. I opened the door and leaned inside the van. In a stern voice I declared: "If you kids don't knock it off I'll…" And that's where I stopped, catching myself about to say a stupid dad thing. Suddenly in that moment of silence, Billy looked at me and simply asked, "You'll do what, Dad? You're a parenting instructor." That moment was permanently etched into my memory to act as a guide for better management of my emotions and reactions to the behavior of others. By the early 1990's, my years of searching for the answers on the right way to discipline began to pay off. A series of amazing discoveries and opportunities appeared in my life that would further guide my journey to writing this book. Of those, several are crucial. It started with the discovery of the organization INCAF (International Network for Children and Families). I joined INCAF as a parent educator and began teaching the "Redirecting Children's Behavior" parenting class. I developed a close working relationship with INCAF's president and author of the parenting program, Kathryn Kvols, who shared her great wealth of knowledge. Her leadership and friendship were invaluable to me and a true inspiration. Soon after, I was invited to attend a special training titled "The 7 Habits of Highly Effective People," a leadership training course developed by Dr. Stephen R. Covey in the field of effective living and productivity. A key component was the development of workshops based on the concepts, and to teach it to others through the method known as third-person instruction. One more important event worth mentioning was an experiential workshop known as UYO or "Understanding Yourself and Others." This unique weekend experience from Bill Riedler's Global Relationship Center made such an impact on me that I returned three times. From this experience I learned that I can be powerful without weakening others, I can love with passion, and I can create anything I choose, including the relationships I wanted to have.

While a personal and professional transformation was occurring, I became interested in the research and works of Alfred Adler and Rudolf Dreikurs M.D. As the founder of the school of Individual Psychology, Adler collaborated with Sigmund Freud around the turn of the 20th century and was the first to present a unique concept: The child should be raised in a democratic home.

He believed that helping children feel like they have a place within the family will avoid the development of personality disorders or neurotic conditions such as anxiety or depression as an adult. He also said that parents weren't the only ones responsible for making this shift, but teachers and other professionals who play a role in raising children should also take parent education training to develop these unique skills. American psychiatrist Rudolf Dreikurs took Adler's works one step further. He suggested that children's misbehavior reflects their desire to fit into the family or the classroom. When children feel like valuable contributors to a unit, they are more likely to be cooperative and behave according to standards set respectfully and consistently by the caregivers. It is from this foundation that I have constructed the methodology and principles you will read about in this book and experience in my course work, *Love, Limits and Lessons*®.

My final acknowledgement is to my God for my incredibly rewarding and long life, and for the prayers answered that helped me make it through my childhood and early adulthood safely so that I could be here to write this book and offer what I've learned to others.

# Introduction

The concepts, suggestions, and methods in this book come from many years of learning, experience, and practice as an oldest child, parent, grandparent, parent educator, corporate manager, and step-dad. In all these roles I took the responsibility, as Rudolf Dreikurs suggested, of helping others fit in and find their place within the social unit. The result has been greater cooperation for me in achieving my own personal and team goals, and in building nurturing relationships along the way. I developed and used these to guide and teach my three children, I incorporated them into leadership of my employees, and I have even used them in my marriage.

At this writing, my grandchildren Blaize and Aurora and my teenage stepdaughter Olivia are my test participants, giving me many opportunities to examine and refine my concepts and practices. If you're reading this as a parent participant in the *Love, Limits, and Lessons®* parenting class, it will act as a guide to help you sharpen your parenting skills and build your courage. If you are a general reader, you will learn that this methodology is not just about getting the kids to behave. What you will learn are suggested practices for discipline that will assist you in gaining greater cooperation from your children today while putting them in touch with their inner guidance system. It is their inner voice that is waiting to be heard and to guide them toward their true purpose in life.

In my writing, you will notice that when I refer to the child, I will alternate genders; he and she, or between her and him regularly. I want to be clear that in no way do I connect one gender over the other to a specific behavior or a solution. This alternating reference is simply a way for me to generally refer to the child and keep my writing smooth.

There is a multitude of parenting books on the market today, and many of them provide in-depth information on behaviors, motivations, temperaments and approaches to help a parent conquer the more challenging behaviors.  I purposely constructed this book in a much different fashion, providing parents with topics they want help with immediately.  Most of the topics are based on the top questions I get at my seminars and workshops. Thus, you will be able to read it from beginning to end, or turn to a specific scenario or situation and get the help you need quickly.

One final thought:  A friend once asked me to get involved in a social organization dedicated to advancing the cause of world peace.  He told me my help was needed at rallies, making and holding signs, and using my speaking skills to reach more people to spread the message.  I thanked him and declined the offer.  While I certainly support the principle of greater world peace, I do not support achieving it by disrupting lives with protests or acting superior to others.  Instead, it is my belief that making the world a better place to live begins at home as effective and powerful, democratic parents.  It is through this style of parenting that we'll raise a generation of responsible and emotionally intelligent children who will seek and find their place in this world, and then move it forward.

# The Five Ways Children Learn

The behavior a child demonstrates is the product of his natural traits, combined with what he has learned from the world around him. A child who acts respectfully and cooperates freely has been treated respectfully, or has seen models of respectful behavior. Frustrating and challenging behavior demonstrated by a child is an attempt to tell the adults that she has not found her place to fit in yet, or is imitating inappropriate behavior to have her needs met. While parents do not have the power to change a child's traits, they can influence a child's learning by creating an environment filled with opportunity that will result in the behavior they want from the child. There are five ways a child learns how to behave: Observations, results of behavior, instruction, positive reinforcement, and thought process.

**Observations.** Children learn from what they see in the world around them and they take in more than you may realize. At times when you think your child is busy playing, he is listening to and observing the activities of others, even if not actively engaged in the discussion or activity. A big part of learning is to copy, imitate and duplicate to "try things on" for size. As all parents know, what they say or do in the presence of their child provides examples to follow. A child's observations also include other children at play, adult interactions, television and video, and general behavior they see out in public.

**Results of Behavior.** The impact of children's behavior presents a valuable lesson that may guide them in knowing what they should repeat and what they should not. More importantly, the reaction of the parent or teacher to the behavior can help the child see the lesson being presented more clearly, or rob her of the experience. The mother of a preschooler contacted me about a problem with her daughter. The little girl was becoming too bossy with playmates and before too long, no one wanted to play with her. Without having good parent coaching skills, the mom wasn't able to help her daughter see that the problem directly resulted from her behavior. Instead, mom faulted the other children and began to search for more playmates for her daughter.

**Instruction.** Children need to know what positive and acceptable behavior looks like. They don't arrive in the world with all this knowledge; they need good instruction to help them learn and cope. Instruction involves creating rules and boundaries, and setting things up in advance so that children have clear instructions before an activity begins. I have always created guidelines for events and activities — rules for the weekend, the summer, a party, visiting, and even about the use of my things. Creating rules isn't a result of a parent's autocratic power; the rules should be created with the children. Before going into a grocery store with my granddaughter, I would get down on one knee so that I am at her eye level. In a playful tone, I would invite her to help me come up with the rules for entering the store. One time she offered the first rule: "No singing out loud." Trying to keep from laughing, I thanked her for coming up with such a great rule. I then added a few more, the ones I really wanted, such as cooperation to remain seated in the shopping carriage and avoiding buying sweets.

**Positive Reinforcement.** When my children were young and behaved in a cooperative and appropriate manner, I would get down to their eye level (do you see a theme here?) and make a big deal of thanking them and letting them know how helpful they were to me. I would do this in an animated manner. The more I did this, the more I achieved the behavior I wanted. Children do things if there is a payoff, and they will respond most effectively to positive reinforcement that helps them feel valued and important. They truly want to be noticed by the adult caregiver and to please them. Often, children hear a "potty" word and out of curiosity, begin using it. If the reaction of the adults is one of shock and anger, the child may "get stuck" in using it more often than he should. I encourage parents to play down the use of the potty word by simply declaring a rule about not allowing it to be used. Then, help the child come up with a more appropriate but amusing word for them to say instead. Whenever the child uses the approved word, the parent should be excited and animated in expressions of support about its use. When my grandson went through one of these phases, I pretended that his use of the new approved word hurt my ears and I ran from him, covering my ears with excitement. He would chase me yelling the new word, just to have fun.

**Thought Process**. The final way children learn is their reaction following a moment of learning, an incident, or a behavior demonstrated by themselves or others. During these moments of thought, children process what happened and formulate assessments and make decisions about themselves and others. If their self-concept is positive and with coaching from the parent, children can make remarkably powerful decisions that will help shape their values and set a foundation for their future behavior.

# The Ten Ways Parents Teach

The word discipline is a variation of the word disciple, which means student or follower. It is my belief that a parent or teacher must strive to teach children many positive lessons as they grow. Discipline must never involve getting even with the child, making her pay for bad behavior, making her feel regret, or showing who's the boss. What we must teach them through discipline includes: how to meet their needs appropriately, hear their inner voice for guidance and encouragement, to be self-sufficient, to draw boundaries, to create positive relationships, to solve their own problems, to take care of themselves, and more. The concepts and methods you will learn are designed to treat the child with fairness and respect, using unconditional love.

The most effective ways of teaching children through discipline in today's world differ greatly from the methods used by our parents. Because of this, they can be challenging for some adults to grasp and master. Here are ten powerful ways to teach children.

**Lecturing**. This method usually comes naturally to many adults and is one that was modeled poorly by our parents. Used inappropriately, it tends to be one-way communication for parental expression of condescending tones and language. Used in an effective way however, it can instruct and guide the child, but requires some fun and creativity to ensure the child is listening. This is especially important for children approaching or in adolescence, when they feel they know more than adults. One method is to set up the lecture by asking for the child's permission to say a "silly dad thing." Another is to announce that I am about to offer a set of "Dad's Rules of Life," or for my stepdaughter, "Bill's

Rules of Life." I get the rolling eyes either way, but I know they are listening. Sometimes I've given lectures that were disguised as offering my opinion on a general situation to the other parent, while the child is close by and within listening range. I once wanted to give my stepdaughter an important message on keeping herself safe, but I knew that she might reject the offering at that time. Instead, I waited until the three of us were in the same room and I began to give my opinion on a situation to my wife, so that my stepdaughter could hear. I winked so that my wife would get the message. My stepdaughter listened without any opposition.

**Feedback**. Similar to a lecture, feedback consists of comments and guidance offered to the child by the parent following an incident or experience. The comments may be suggestions on how to handle a situation differently in the future or simply the parent's observations on what they saw. Feedback may also be recognition or "kudos" to the child for handling something well. Positive reinforcement should always be used when your child behaves in ways that you want her to, regardless of her age — such as when she pushes in her chair, puts her toys away, or plays nicely with her brother. The parent should always be on the lookout for positive behavior and be ready to make a big deal out of it. For toddlers and preschoolers, the feedback should be dramatic, animated and offered in an excited tone to let the child know what a great job he did. The drama and animation should be reduced for school-age children and eliminated of course, for teens. When my son was in his teens, I would approach him casually, offer the encouragement about something he did in a sincere but low-key tone, and then walk away.

**Consequences**. There are two types of consequences: natural and logical. Natural consequences are the direct results of a child's behavior when an adult does not intervene to rescue, punish, or scold. The child is confronted with the results of his behavior and learns from it. For example, a child does not take responsibility for remembering to take his project to school and calls the parent to bring it to him. The parent declines and the child is faced with a low grade. The child learns to remember his school work in the future.                     The natural consequence is not appropriate for all situations. There may be a need for the parent to create a logical consequence with the child in advance, or implement one after the fact due to inappropriate behavior. For example, a child receives a new bicycle for her birthday and to keep her safe, mom sets up safety rules for riding the bike in the yard. If she rides too close to the road, the consequence developed in advance may be that she loses the privilege of riding for the rest of the day. In another situation, the child speaks rudely to her father, causing her dad to feel hurt. The consequence might be that dad decides not to bring her on a planned visit to the mall. The daughter learns to consider the feelings of others before speaking disrespectfully. For more helpful information on creating and implementing consequences, see the chapter that covers that topic.

**Rules**. Parents are responsible for ensuring their children's safety, teaching responsibility, and helping children understand preserving the rights of others. Setting up rules in advance is an effective tool and can be used to increase successful outcomes of experiences and events. Rules are also more effective if they are developed with the children. When my children were young, I had a pool installed and purchased a trampoline for our fenced-in backyard. I wanted to get to know my kids' friends so my goal was to create an enjoyable place for the friends to visit more often. The first thing we did was to sit down as a family and develop a list of the rules for having friends over and using the back yard. The list included rules for extending invitations, use of the equipment, and general behavior issues. I was amazed when my son offered the rule of no fighting. Don't be surprised by what they come up with when you invite your children to help create rules. When they feel like they have a place in the family, their behavior can change drastically.

**Agreements**. To get their children to cooperate, many parents simply tell or require a child to do something, and then think she should follow through. If the child does not feel like she has a place in the family, or feel valued or respected, she will often sabotage the relationship by not following through with what she was told to do. The secret for achieving cooperation is to explain what the adult needs and then come to an agreement with the child on the details — picking up toys, completing chores, being home at a certain time, etc. What makes the agreement work is not only engaging children respectfully into the discussion, but also asking them to make it final by describing the agreement in their own words. There is more helpful information on agreements in other chapters.

**Living Examples**. You are a living, breathing role model for your children. They will learn more about how to live their lives effectively by watching you, so make sure that you are setting the example that you want them to emulate. And examples should include the behavior of others in public, or actions displayed on television. While getting into the car with my teenage son after a shopping trip, I noticed a man standing on the curb facing a very busy road, holding what appeared to be a walking stick designed especially for the visually impaired. My fear was that he was about to step into the road and endanger himself. I told my son I would be right back and I headed over to the gentleman. I asked him if he needed any help and he revealed that he was confused and couldn't find the bus stop. I told him that he was a few hundred feet from the bus stop and asked him how I could best help him get there. He asked me to lead him by talking and he would follow my voice. When I returned to the car my son said, "That was cool, dad."

**Asking Questions.** Our children are smarter than we give them credit for. We are so worried that they are not going to do what is right, or we are in such a hurry that it just seems easier to give our children marching orders. But asking them questions is a far more effective teaching tool. Often, they know exactly what to do and when they come up with solutions to their own questions or challenges, it builds their problem-solving skills. I always encourage parents to refrain from telling their children what to do or from answering their questions so quickly. Instead, ask them questions such as "what do you think?" "what will you do now?" "what did you notice?" Asking children questions also builds their own confidence and strengthens their faith in themselves.

**Coaching.** Taking the art of asking questions one step further, coaching adds two more elements that teach a child greater problem-solving skills: Telling a child what you see, and offering to help. Putting these three concepts together creates a powerful method for parenting that will build the child's coping skills. You are not always going to be at your children's side to protect them, so you have to arm them with the ability to cope and survive. Telling your children what you see provides a perspective that they can compare to their own assessment. Asking them questions invites creativity and solutions. And finally, offering to help gives them the courage to take on things that they might feel are too big for them; whether it's putting on a bandage, choosing a book report project, or finding solutions to teen problems.

**Living Out Loud**. Similar to living by example, this concept takes teaching one step further and works best with younger children. By living out loud, you seek opportunities to set an example by narrating what you're doing. For example, you are watching television and your child is playing in the same room. You want your child to learn that television is not what life is all about and that it should be limited, so as you turn it off you say out loud for anyone to hear: "That's enough television for me today." If your spouse does something for you that demonstrates respect, say out loud: "I love it when mommy gets me a glass of water." If you're serving the meal and your child is at the table and watching, you could say: "Everyone gets a small serving of pasta because they need to leave room for the vegetables." Using this narration will teach many wonderful messages about respectful living, boundaries and limits.

**Accomplishments**. One final method for teaching your children is through the examples of your actions and individual accomplishments that will speak to them for many years. It is more than living by example and the things you do on a regular basis. It is about what you create that influences others. I think of these things as "our works" that contribute to making the world a better place to live. Doing so teaches children important lessons about the power we each have to give back to the world, and inspires them to do the same.

# Six Irrefutable Laws about Kids

Much of the frustration we experience with our children's behavior is caused by a lack of understanding kids. Expanding our thinking about our children and accepting some basic, rudimentary facts will help us change the way we see their behavior and also change our behavior as a parent. We will be much more successful as caregivers if we see the world from our child's point of view. Here are six irrefutable laws about kids that will change the way we use discipline.

**They Live Only In The Moment.** Whatever the young child happens to be doing at the moment is his entire world. His full attention and focus is on the activity in front of him and he is usually unable to think about anything else unless another activity offers more incentive than the current activity.

**What Adults Can Do:**
- Establish rules prior to the start of each activity
- Use visual timers to create limits for some activities
- Be patient when moving him from one activity to another
- Point out "what's in it for him" in the next activity

**They Don't Care About Order and Cleanliness.** It drives us crazy when our child won't pick up her toys when she's finished playing with them, or when she's thirteen and seems perfectly fine living in a bedroom that is in total disarray. Forcing her to clean things up by yelling and punishing doesn't work and can harm our relationship with her.

**What Adults Can Do:**
- Relax and make cleanup fun

- Demonstrate excitement when it does occur
- Set up agreements prior to the start of an activity
- If the child doesn't follow thru, guide them back silently and respectfully

**They Get Frustrated Very Easily.** There are a few things that cause children to become frustrated, resulting in tantrums and meltdowns; wanting to be just like us and do what we do, becoming easily overcome by the physical effects of fatigue, hunger, and illness, and a lack of firm and consistent boundaries. When we say, "No cookies before dinner," and then give in, we are actually teaching them to have meltdowns to get us to give in more often.

**What Adults Can Do:**
- Be patient and help them address what is causing the frustration
- Detach from their emotion and be there with them in silence
- Let them be frustrated without reprimanding or sending them to timeout
- Avoid caving in to their demands to break a boundary or limit

**They Learn By Testing Our Boundaries.** One day, when my daughter was a preschooler, I drew a chalk line across the driveway to mark the farthest point she could ride her new tricycle to keep her a safe distance from the street. I explained to her the consequence of breaking this boundary was the loss of her tricycle for the remainder of the day. With a twinkle in her eye, she crossed the line one day to see what I would do. Immediately, I silently and gently took her tricycle from her and hung it on a hook in the garage. It broke my heart to watch her cry, but she didn't get it back until the following day.

**What Adults Can Do:**
- Accept children's testing as normal and not misbehavior
- Set clear and consistent boundaries and keep them in place
- Create consequences that are related to the infraction
- React without emotion and in silence

**They Need to Feel Powerful.** Every human strives to feel a sense of power and value within the social unit to which they belong. Employees work more collaboratively when they clearly know what their role is on a work team, athletes perform better when they know what position they play on the sports team, and children become more cooperative when they feel a sense of power in the family or the classroom. A successful leader as a manager, a coach, a parent, or a teacher helps the members of the social unit feel powerful in appropriate ways.

**What Adults Can Do:**
- Provide appropriate ways for children to feel powerful
- Allow the child to teach the adult something
- Find creative ways to allow the child to be the boss of something
- Let the child take a turn at being the family meeting facilitator

**They Don't Always Like Their Playmate or Sibling.** When a playmate begins to hit another child, it is basically a message to the caregiver that she has had enough of the other child. Because of their egocentric point of view, small children do not naturally like to share and they also see the other child as a threat to the supply of love and attention they receive from the adult caregivers.

What Adults Can Do:
- Avoid putting a child in timeout for hitting or not getting along
- Use modeling to teach small children how to share, not by force
- Be sure that adult relationships around the child demonstrate kindness
- Allow each child to have alone time away from playmates or siblings

# Two Forms of Discipline –

# Preventive and Fire Fighting

We can take two approaches to anything that we dedicate ourselves to maintain in our lives: proactive steps to avoid emergencies and reactive steps to handle the emergency when it occurs. Let's examine our health. The proactive steps, or what I call preventive measures, are exercising regularly, implementing smart eating habits, and getting regular check-ups with our primary care physician. When we don't do this on a regular basis, we risk a health-related emergency that could cause us to have to take reactive actions, or what I call fire fighting measures — drastic means to bring our health back or to just stay alive.

In our world of finance, we know that we should be using preventive measures by making regular deposits in our various financial accounts, paying our creditors regularly, and keeping a watchful eye on our credit. When we let it all slip and a financial emergency occurs, we must react with a fire fighting solution to find more money, seek financial assistance, or sell our possessions.

We could not exist in this world without our relationships. We need others to care for us, to love us, to work for and with us, and to help us achieve our objectives and goals. Preventive maintenance of our relationships means checking in with people, providing things for others, letting them know we care, mentoring, and so on. But, when we get too busy and don't use the preventive measures that keep us connected, we may see emergency situations occur in our relationships such as backbiting, avoidance, sabotage, or abandonment of the relationship. This could require fire fighting actions to save the relationship such as making amends and apologies to others, or finding replacements and having to start over.

Have you noticed that the actions are different? Preventive discipline action items are completely different from fire fighting discipline action items. The actions you would take as preventive measures on your car, such as regular oil changes, tune-ups, and gasoline fill-ups, are not the same actions you would take to implement fire fighting measures if it stopped running.

Understanding and using this preventive vs. fire fighting approach to anything in life, results in action plans for preventive management. This reduces the chances of more costly and difficult fire fighting actions required to save or repair what we have.

Raising and disciplining children requires the same approach. Fire fighting discipline methods are actions a parent takes when the child is misbehaving and uncooperative. At this point, we are at our wits' end, ready to call for help, send our kids to the zoo, or find a parenting class. Preventive discipline methods are actions a parent takes the rest of the time; when the children are NOT misbehaving. It is difficult because it requires proactive measures when the kids are behaving well. Usually when our children are cooperative and calm, we use this time to avoid disturbing them and to get things done. But the fact is, if we spend more time using preventive discipline methods, we'll spend less time using fire fighting methods.

The following chapters in this book are designed to help with specific situations. They each address a problem, provide an understanding of the issue, give examples, and then describe solutions to help you deal effectively with the situation. At the end of each chapter you will also find a Parents Preventive Action Plan to begin implementing immediately.

Handling frustrating and challenging behavior in your children can be extremely stressful. You just want it to stop. It may also be difficult for you to see clearly what the preventive discipline should be to reduce or stop it. First determine the root cause of the challenging behavior by seeking out patterns and triggers that signal the onset of the problem. Here are some questions to ask yourself:

- What is my child trying to tell me with this behavior?

- What need is my child expressing at the moment?

- What was going on with my child just before the behavior began?

- What was going on with me just prior to the problem?

- What is it I feel when I am confronted with the behavior?

- What measures can I take in the future to avoid the challenging behavior?

# Are Children Today Really More of a Challenge?

I do believe that raising children today is a much greater challenge than it was for previous generations, but it's not the child that is the problem. Instead, the causes are circumstances that we as parents can control. As a discipline specialist working with today's families, I've noticed a couple of factors that contribute to the challenge of raising children today.

First of all, it's a different world today than it was for past generations: Information is quick and access is easy, communication travels faster, money is more readily available, and there are so many more conveniences available to us. This compels us to feel that we must accomplish more, acquire more, and be more competitive. Raising children effectively requires parents to be more patient and to make an effort to take care of themselves physically, emotionally, and spiritually... greater challenges in today's "microwave" world.

Today's faster-paced lifestyle increases the stress level of parents, makes it difficult to live more consciously, and leads to a reduced presence for our children. While we may be with our children and spouses physically, our attention and thoughts are elsewhere. And they may end up feeling totally disconnected from us. We wind up with children who are starved for our attention and do whatever it takes to get it, even if it risks verbal punishment.

**Changes in the Family Structure**. Changes in the family structure reflecting an increased divorce rate result in greater numbers of single-parent families. With more financial strain on families today, many parents are working multiple jobs to earn the income necessary to make ends meet. When you combine the two — a single custodial parent working multiple jobs - the strain on the parent/child relationship increases astronomically.

**Parenting Style**. The styles of parenting have changed over the years. Many parents have come to the conclusion that punishment does not work and have adopted alternative positive-parenting discipline. Still others avoid using discipline completely because they remember the impact of being punished on their self-image and their relationship with their parents. The drawback to more alternatives is that some parents become confused and utilize an unstructured method that can create a new set of problems. When past generations used authoritarian parenting styles and tools such as traditional punishment and admonition, children were easier to handle because they were under the parents' control. But when controlling methods are not used, the control passes back to the child. The results are frustrating, stressful and tiresome to parents who are already over-burdened by today's life and work styles.

**Structure and Routine**. One more final contributor could be defined as structure and routine, a requirement and a learning experience for children. In past generations, there were many more rules, boundaries, and expectations. For example, fathers consistently returned each day at an expected hour, the family came together each evening at suppertime, and Sundays were reserved as family time. There are fewer procedures and routines in today's family and, in many cases, much more disorder. This discord is adopted by the children in the family, making life more chaotic for today's parents. Many of them were reared in homes where parents were in control. Their current lack of control over their children produces a feeling of being lost.

**Reconnect and Change**. To reconnect and change your family dynamics, slow down. Don't try to do everything. You can make this change by:
- Being more consistent in your parenting and discipline.
- Holding regular family meetings.
- Restoring the evening family meal time.

- Using less punishment and more positive principles of parenting.
- Listening to your children when they talk – learning to be fully present.
- Living your daily life with the recognition that you are a model for your children.

Finally, take good care of yourself. Strong and effective parenting today begins with proper eating, plenty of sleep and exercise, and focusing on your spirituality. If you do this, a foundation is created for building the patience and strength necessary for rearing well-rounded children in today's fast-paced world.

# Those Annoying (But Normal) Behaviors

I was standing in line at a small-town general store behind a mom with her preteen daughter and a little boy who appeared to be about 2. He was eye-level with a wall full of candy boxes and kept picking up pieces packaged in the shiniest wrappers. Each time he picked one up he just wanted to touch it to see it sparkling and crinkling. And each time his mom would turn around from her transaction at the register and snap at him not to touch. She snatched away the candy, put it back and then snapped "No!" In response, he whimpered, picked up another piece of candy from a different box and the same routine would play out; mom would yell at him and take it away. She finally lost her cool, picked him up and shouted, "No! We do not touch!" As she put him back down on the floor he started to cry, immediately went to another display just out of her reach and picked something else up from the shelf. She looked at me briefly in embarrassment. I smiled and told her, "They just want to touch everything, don't they? I've found that if you give them something to hold that you're OK with, they're easier to manage in a store with so many things to touch." She smiled back and reached into her purse, pulled out a handful of connected keys and key chains, and handed them to him. His whimpering stopped as he suddenly became fascinated with the keys, mumbling to himself in a satisfied way. She thanked me and scurried out of the store, her arms filled with groceries, ushering her two children in front of her. On the way out, the little boy was still mesmerized by the shiny metal in his little hands.

This classic scenario is an example of normal behavior that is difficult to deal with. Whether we like it or not, our children are wired to touch, poke, and play with everything around them. That's how they learn and develop, through exploration and discovery.

And how frustrated I feel for the adult and the child when I see the parent snapping, yelling, and sometimes even spanking to punish him for what he is harmlessly motivated to do.

Let's not be so quick to blame the parent in my scenario. It was around 4 p.m. when I saw her in the general store, and she probably had a lot on her mind. Dinner may have been late, she was shopping for items needed for the meal, she was probably tired and impatient, and it appeared that her preteen daughter may have been talking her ear off while standing in line at the register. And why did she snap and eventually shout at her little son? Perhaps she was experiencing a combination of feelings: Frustrated that her son was not standing cooperatively by her side, overwhelmed with all that was preying on her mind, annoyed that her son was getting into things, and embarrassed that she may have made a negative impression as a parent to others waiting in line.

Hindsight is 20/20, as they say, and my suggestion was easy, but when we learn to recognize normal behaviors in our children and are prepared to deal with them when they occur, our lives can be less stressful. A child misbehaves because she has needs. Once we learn to recognize those needs when they appear and develop a method to help meet her needs on our terms, life is less complicated.

As reflected in the scenario above, the little boy's need was to touch and explore. Had his mother been prepared to recognize this and to provide him with something he could touch and play with, the harsh encounter might have been avoided. We all feel regret when we yell at our children or spank them. It tarnishes the unconditional love we want them to feel from us and causes us to feel guilt for our actions and our words. We do it because we lack the alternatives to resolve the issue.

When my granddaughter was a toddler, she loved catching me off-guard at shopping malls until I learned to be more prepared. Being just out of reach, with a mischievous look in her eye, she would run away while looking back to be sure that I was in pursuit. And of course, I wasn't chasing her to have fun; instead, I was dreading awful outcomes resulting in her being grabbed or lost in the crowd. She loved the game; her need was to play with me and to get me to chase her. So, understanding her needs, I developed a strategy. As soon as I took her from her car seat, I got down to her eye level and told her that we would frolic in the play area. To get there, she could either hold my hand or ride on my shoulders. Recognizing her needs in advance and setting up the safety boundaries increased her cooperation; my mall excursions with her more successful.

# Interpreting Misbehavior

Before imposing discipline on their children, I always ask the adults in my parenting classes to carefully examine and understand the behavior they are trying to stop. I explain that a lot of what we might label as misbehavior falls into one of five categories: learned behavior, exploration, communication, getting needs met, and an emotional bank account on overdraft. Sometimes it can be stopped by first understanding the root cause and dealing with that. Let's examine each of these in more detail.

**Learned Behavior.** Learned behavior is something children demonstrate that they have seen somewhere and then repeat. Children absorb so much by watching and listening to the adults (and other children) around them. A young woman approached me following one of my seminars and asked what she should do when her 5-year-old daughter screams "No!" at her. When I asked her how she usually says "no" to her daughter, she looked at me in shock and exclaimed, "Oh my gosh!" She realized that she was the one who had taught her child this behavior. As a volunteer speaker for the Department of Corrections, I conducted workshops for incarcerated fathers on the impact of their behavior on their children. I told them that their little sons will learn how to treat little girls by the example set by their fathers toward their mothers. I also explained that their daughters will learn to accept the kind of treatment they see their fathers exhibiting toward their mothers. Often, we can correct a child's "learned" behavior by simply teaching new lessons and creating different models for them.

**Exploration.** Sometimes a child's behavior appears to us as misbehavior when in fact it is his way of learning about the world around him. Children are wired by nature to explore and discover, but their exploration can frustrate and annoy us, causing us to want to stop it. Our objective should be to accept the child's need to explore and then create boundaries for them to carry it out. After closing my talk to a group of toddlers' moms a few years ago, one young woman asked me how to prevent her son from flushing things down the toilet. I helped her recognize the exploration and discovery he was demonstrating, and encouraged her to channel that natural desire in more appropriate ways. I also encouraged her to realize that her young son saw the toilet as a very mysterious appliance in the house — things go down and then magically disappear. There was no need to punish this behavior. Instead, I encouraged her to demonstrate where the objects belonged, the appropriate use of the toilet, and to show him new avenues of exploration. I cautioned her that if she continued to punish him, his natural curiosity and desire to explore his world could be shot down. Over time, her son's desire to explore could be snuffed out, destroying this critical ingredient for pursuit of his dreams as an adult.

**Communication**. Have you ever seen a parent set an unexpected limit for a child and then watch the child throw a fit? Chances are the child is trying to communicate: "I don't like your sudden change! I feel very small and helpless, and right now I don't like you!" The worst thing a parent can do in this situation is to reprimand the child. Instead, the child should be allowed to express her frustration and anger. One day my pre-teenaged son ran into the house and asked permission to make some popcorn to take back to a neighbor's house where he and a friend were watching a movie. When he revealed to me the title of the "PG-13" rated movie they were watching, I could not let him return to the neighbor's home until I had had a chance to talk to that boy's parents. I apparently had not done a great job communicating to the neighbor my boundaries for acceptable movies to be watched by my children. My son became very angry with me, rightfully so in view of my sudden change in his activity with no advance notice.

**Getting Needs Met**. A child may demonstrate apparent

misbehavior simply to satisfy unfulfilled needs. We all know that children need such basics as love, hugs, clothing, warmth, health care, a roof over their heads, and food. We often lack awareness of other needs such as a desire to feel important, powerful, heard and understood. A desire to meet those needs can lead to acting-out behavior. Child psychologist Dr. Rudolf Dreikurs wrote in his book *Children The Challenge* (Plume; 1991) that in order for parents to successfully discipline their children, they must first understand that much misbehavior is an effort to have their needs met. Dreikurs defines what the specific needs are, and many are discussed later in this book. Taking a parenting course like Love, Limits and Lessons will help you understand how your child's genuine needs are revealed through their behavior.

**The Emotional Bank Account**. A more successful effort to have children listen and cooperate requires an understanding of something that is missing from most adults' daily focus; making more emotional deposits than withdrawals. In his book *The 7 Habits of Highly Effective People* (Free Press), Steven Covey called it the "emotional bank account". Dr. Tim Jordan talks about the "goodwill account" in his book *Keeping Your Kids Grounded When You're Flying by the Seat of Your Pants* (Palmerston & Reed). Like a financial bank account, this "account" with your child is an internal repository that requires daily deposits and a minimum amount of withdrawals to keep the balance high. When it is kept high, a child is more likely to cooperate with and listen to the adult who is making the deposits. A child has separate accounts for each adult in their life.

Deposits are examples of an adult's verbal and active demonstrations of love for the child. Deposits include keeping promises, giving frequent hugs and kisses, speaking respectfully, spending time with them, doing things that help the child feel heard and understood, letting them have a say in family matters, involving them in creating consequences, and employing more techniques for encouragement rather than praise. Withdrawals involve actions and words that actually withhold love from another person. Among the examples: Yelling, hitting, lying, blaming, name-calling, denying, breaking promises, being distant, making assumptions, and being unavailable.

Imagine a relationship with someone who is constantly

taking withdrawals from your emotional bank account but making very few deposits. Now try to imagine your feelings toward that person. Do you think you would be cooperative, caring and supportive of their desires and needs? Most likely, you would attempt to sabotage the relationship or avoid that person all together if possible. You might even attempt to leave the relationship. Now imagine being in a different relationship with someone who makes more deposits than withdrawals. Can you imagine how you would feel and act differently? Would you drop everything to assist them when help was needed? Would you want to go out of your way to be there for them? How full do you think the emotional bank account is between you and your child at this moment? Have you been making enough deposits to get the cooperation you need?

Today's fast-paced lifestyle keeps us moving quickly with so much to accomplish daily. We wear so many different hats that require us to complete tasks faster and more efficiently. Some of us also get so preoccupied with seeking the best schools, the best gadgets and the best opportunities for our children that we lose sight of the more important priorities — ourselves, our time, and our attention. What seems to be at the root of much misbehavior today is the absence of a daily emotional connection between parents and children.

I encourage you to begin making more deposits in your child's emotional bank account today by slowing down your pace and taking note of the simple things that your child does that delight you. Take the time to acknowledge good behavior and give encouraging comments often, not just praise. Because we are human, we will make mistakes and make withdrawals more often than we would like. Your first step is to catch yourself making them and admit it. The next step is to make at least 3 deposits within a reasonable time frame to counter the effects of that one withdrawal. And don't stop with your child; make extra deposits in your significant other's emotional bank account as well, and watch the relationship grow stronger and more loving!

# Teaching Boundaries - Getting Started

A woman I know allowed her 9-year-old daughter to have a friend sleep over during the holidays. When she was pouring her coffee the next morning, her little guest walked into the kitchen and asked, "Can I have some coffee?" The mother denied her request and was informed by the child of the many other adult-type privileges and rituals she was allowed at her home. Based on what the little girl revealed, it was obvious to the woman that this child lived in an environment with very few boundaries; in fact, her mom was treating her more as an adult girl-friend and less as a child.

Many years ago when my middle daughter was around the same age and had a friend sleep over, her friend unpacked a couple of movies to watch. After a close examination, I told our little house guest that I did not approve showing those videos in our home. I was familiar with two of them and the content was not, in my opinion, at all appropriate for my children. The third was a movie I had not yet seen and could not allow them to watch it because I had not. I always previewed movies before I would allow my children to see them on the assumption that they were not Disney-type animation. My daughter's friend declared that it was all right because her mom lets her watch PG- and R-rated movies. I stood by my rules and the videos were not played.

I have a big concern about parents who have few or no boundaries for their children and expose them prematurely to adult material. I am appalled when I see young children at a theater showing a movie with violence or sex. I have even had some parents tell me that I'm too old-fashioned, prudish or paranoid. Some parents who find it "too difficult" to filter content for their children argue that "they are going to see (or experience) it somewhere, so why make life difficult for myself." My personal philosophy has been that if I create clear, defined rules and boundaries up front for my children, they will take me seriously as a parent and discipline will be easier as they grow. But if we become too lax in our parenting, a slippery slope develops as they get older, and we soon begin losing control. I made it a point to preserve my kids' childhoods to allow them to fully enjoy this innocent, limited time of exploration, self-discovery and emotional growth. I wanted them to complete their development as children before reaching the next cycle of change.

Boundaries are critical learning tools for children. Here are three simple suggestions you can implement immediately.

**House Rules**. All children need boundaries and limits as models for learning. A good starting point involves general house rules that apply to children as young as pre-schoolers. Just conducting this respectful discussion will help them feel that they are a part of the family and can contribute by adopting your rules. In a family meeting, sit down with your children and discuss areas that need some boundaries, such as greeting one another, use and management of coats and shoes, use of electronics and the telephone, bedtimes, and friends. If you have a child old enough to write, allow them to serve as the meeting scribe to record all the rules. Once the list is completed (don't make it too complex), have it read aloud; then, everyone signs it. As a reminder, the rules can be posted in a prominent spot.

**Chores**. Children as young as pre-schoolers can be assigned chores to help out around the house. It begins to teach them responsibility and acceptable behaviors. Select another family meeting setting and let the children know you'll be discussing chores. Encourage their involvement in the discussion by asking them how they could help out. Obviously, pre-schoolers might have one or two very simple jobs. School-age children can have about a half-dozen. Keep the items simple and easy to track, and be sure that some of them include picking up after themselves. Some examples: Making their bed, setting the table, putting away their laundry, folding towels and filling up the dog-food dish. I have never paid my children an allowance for these types of tasks; I have told them that these are required for family membership. I've also told them that this list of daily or weekly chores represents cooperation with the parents, and when we get cooperation regularly, we are more likely to want to cooperate when they want something. That might mean bringing them to a friend's house to play, taking them to a movie or out to eat, or planning extra fun on the weekend. To keep them on track, create a list of the chores that can be checked off each day as they are completed. Acknowledge them for cooperating and completing them as planned.

**Limiting Entertainment Electronics**. I suggest putting limitations on children's exposure to television, video games and non-academic computer activities. Limiting them to perhaps one hour a day on school days and two hours on weekend days will teach them about moderation when it comes to entertainment. Parents have told me countless stories about how, following their children's initial anger over the change, they watched them rediscover the lost art of playing, creating, and reading when electronics-time was ended for the day. As a parent myself, I have observed these time limits as a standard rule. But with any rule that I set up, I have always advised children that as the parent, I reserve the right to modify the rule on the fly if necessary. In the case of electronics, I may award bonus time because of special circumstances such as having company or as a reward for outstanding cooperation. I also reserve the right to reduce the daily time limitations because of a lack of cooperation. And while my children eventually became responsible for tracking their own time, they were required to always ask for permission to begin the daily allotment. The use of entertainment electronics time is not a right, it is a privilege.

# Setting Limits to Help Children Grow

One day in 1994, my 9-year-old daughter called me at my office to tell me that she had left her lunch money at home again and needed me to bring it to her. This typical forgetfulness by my children was quite annoying but something I thought I was supposed to resolve as a father. On my ride to the school, I couldn't help but think about the inconvenience. More importantly, I suddenly became concerned about how responsible my daughter would eventually be as an adult if I was constantly remembering for her or rescuing her.

That evening, I gathered my three children for an impromptu family meeting to discuss a few changes that would take effect immediately. I announced that from now on, they were solely responsible for remembering to bring with them any items they needed for school that day — lunch money, homework, and school projects. I advised them that unless it was required for health and safety reasons, I was no longer willing to run home and retrieve what they left behind. My responsibility as a dad teaching his children about limits required me to draw a personal boundary. During that meeting, I also took the time to help them come up with ideas that would enable and empower them to remember on their own.

For the next few weeks, my plan worked and the kids were so proud of themselves with their new sense of responsibility — until one day, my 9-year-old daughter called the office. Expressing worry and distress, she told me she had left a book report poster due that day on the dining room table. She described to me how much time and effort she had spent working on it the night before. She then confirmed that she was aware of my new "dad rule" about leaving things at home, but pleaded with me to bring it to her or she would receive a bad grade on the assignment. She promised that this would be the last time that she would ever call me for anything like this. My initial feeling at that moment was that I could go and get it for her, "just this one time," because I loved her so much and didn't want her to fail. But I knew that doing so would violate my boundary and teach her that limits are set to be broken. One of the hardest moments while raising our kids was my decision to tell her that I was abiding by the new family rule, and I was unwilling to retrieve the poster. I wished her a good day, hung up the phone, and cried in my office. As it turned it out, the teacher agreed to give her partial credit for the assignment if she brought it in the very next day; my daughter remembered for herself from that moment on.

Shortly after that incident, I was teaching our children about financial responsibility. At times, I would find it stressful to make sure that I had the correct change and dollar bills in my pocket at the end of the day to give each child the exact amount for lunch money for the next school day. After some discussion with the kids, I decided they were ready for more responsibility so a new rule was set up; I would give each child his lunch money on Sunday nights for the week. They were now responsible for paying for their lunch each day. For some reason, our particular school system would not accept lunch payment in advance for the week so this created a unique challenge. In our discussion about the new rule, I decided that if they lost their lunch money, I would not replace it, and they would have to bring something from home to eat that day — consisting only of a peanut butter and jelly sandwich, crackers with peanut butter, or fruit if available. The point was that if they lost their lunch money, it would not be my requirement to prepare something to eat; that was their responsibility. I was also unwilling to be responsible for purchasing any special foods or making anything. They could bring a lunch that they could make on their own — something that I approved. I do know that some parents thought I was a mean father for taking this approach, but my goal was to develop responsible and capable children.

One evening at home, my son entered the kitchen dragging a dining room chair over to the counter. We had a few friends visiting and he excused himself to clear a path as the adults moved out of this way. He stepped up on the chair and opened the cupboard, taking down a box of crackers and a jar of peanut butter. One of the visitors asked him what he was doing. Without any hesitation, he told them that he had lost his lunch money and was making his lunch for the next day. I got some very strange, judgmental looks. But I had made the decision long ago that I was not in this world to please others or live by their standards. I was a father and I was taking my role very seriously. Today I'm enjoying watching that same little boy as an adult, planning ahead, setting clear boundaries for himself and others, and making wise decisions.

Raising cooperative and responsible children requires teaching them about clear, respectful limits and boundaries. It helps them to become self-sufficient and teaches them personal responsibility. As parents, we love our children dearly, but with our busy schedules and the limited time we have to spend with them, we've become convinced that we need to do more for them, rather than teaching them about limits in advance. And once limits are set up, we have to remember that because our children are wired to explore, they will test those limits. Refrain from punishing your children when they test your boundaries, and remain calm. Realize that if you've done everything for them in the past and have decided to suddenly make changes, their normal reaction may be to push your boundaries even more. Our children want to know "who's flying the plane"; it's up to us to show them we're the pilot!

# Living Out Loud: Teaching by Example

Of all the authors, instructors, and experts I've learned from over the years, the one who taught me the most powerful lessons about effective parenting was my son. He showed me that my daily actions and words were more powerful as a teaching tool than any wisdom I could impart from the experts. My first two children were girls, and they definitely gave me a run for my money as a father. But in 1987 my third and youngest child arrived on the planet and I remember thinking I was well prepared and ready. He challenged me every step of the way, calling me out on things I said and did. By the time he turned 12, I realized how my "Living Out Loud" would end up teaching him, as well as myself, so much more.

One day when my son was about 8, we were driving into town to pick up some supplies at a hardware store. I was rushed for time because the store was about to close. As I rolled through a stop sign, my son asked me, "Dad, weren't you supposed to stop at that sign back there?" I explained to him that we had less than 15 minutes to get to the store before it closed, and I needed to purchase parts for a broken appliance at home. He didn't care about my reason for failing to come to a full stop. Instead, he said, "How am I supposed to learn how to be good driver from you, Dad?" I remember this incident all too well. It stayed with me because it was a turning point in understanding even more strongly how important my role as a father was and how crucial my actions and words were for his growth into a responsible young man.

It's not too late to change our habits and teach our children wonderful life skills they will retain and use over time. I'm talking about things we can say and do that will instruct children about limits and rules by demonstrating our own for them to see and hear. Remember, you are a living, breathing role model for your kids. Demonstrate your own boundaries as learning tools for your children. Here are 6 ways of teaching children limits and boundaries by "Living Out Loud"; what to say and do in front of the kids.

- When you're ready to stop watching television and your children are nearby, say out loud, "That's all the TV I need to watch for now."
- If you realize that you need to stop one activity in favor of another, say: "Mom has to stop making dinner and go put in a load of laundry."
- If someone hurts you, say: "I don't like it when you do that, it hurts me!"
- If the phone is ringing and you don't want to answer it, you could say: "I don't feel like talking on the phone right now because I want to spend time with you."
- Set your alarm clock for the kids to see and tell them, "I need this clock to ring so I will know when sleep time is over and it's time to start my day."
- When you're serving food, say: "I'm going to try a little bit of everything mommy made for dinner, but not too much."

Living out Loud" can also be useful for teaching children about rules for life. While out with our grandchildren one day, we were about to get into the car and I opened the car door for my wife. When I got into the car, I turned to my granddaughter and said, "Here's one of grandpa's rules of life... a polite man always opens the door for a lady so she can get into the car first." I look for frequent opportunities that become teaching moments and ask them, "Can I tell you another one of grandpa's rules of life?" I normally get their confirmation and then proceed to relate a nugget of valuable information. I don't belabor it; just simply give them a bit of information. Then, when they're adults and I'm gone from this world, I hope their children will hear them say, "My grandpa used to say..."

# Why The Kids Won't Listen!

You must have told your child at least a hundred times to bring his lunch box in from the car when the two of you arrived home from school. It seemed like a simple task to teach him responsibility. Getting him to place it on the kitchen counter everyday would make it convenient for you to wash it and repack it the next morning. You are not asking for much and you begin to feel like you have to remember everything for him. It has now become routine for you to notice it missing during your morning rush. You run out to the car in a huff to retrieve it and then yell with frustration about his lack of responsibility. But it happens again and again until you snap and behave in a way that you wish you hadn't. You end up using punishment and getting angry with your child.

Does this scenario sound familiar? Not listening is one of the most common complaints from parents who attend my seminars. It is also a frustrating, common occurrence that sabotages the family and creates chaos at home. Parents then see it as misbehavior and feel that their child is not cooperating. It seems so unfair that you do so much for your child and this is what you get in return. The parent then begins to feel the frustration running over into her marriage. When it doesn't stop there, she begins to feel unappreciated, distracted and unproductive at work; her life feels out of balance.

When a child doesn't listen, I call it parent deafness; the child appears to have tuned out the parent's commands, pleas and requests, and ignores her. In turn, the parent thinks that the child didn't hear the first 50 times, so she repeats her commands over and over again. The result is that the child hears her even less and tunes her out even more. The primary cause of parent deafness is that the adult talks too much. The combination of too much talking, the child's feeling of unimportance and of being overwhelmed with commands while forbidden from demonstrating frustration, can cause the child to ignore the adult and appear not to listen.

One of the even more significant causes of this problem is a child's feeling of emotional disconnection from a very busy parent. Today's high-gear society requires a typical parent to scurry around, anxious about all the tasks at hand; the result is a feeling of stress and over-committed. This type of behavior can cause a child to feel emotionally distant from his parent, creating unresponsiveness to requests. But this can be repaired with some common-sense solutions.

**Reconnect**. Take 5 to 10 minutes a day to reestablish the emotional connection with your children. They want to know that you are there 100 percent, not preoccupied with dinner, bills due, or work schedules. Sit next to them or in front of them and clear your mind. Use direct eye contact and refrain from talking; let them do it all. If you have to speak, ask them questions or react to their comments with simple phrases like: "Wow!" "Tell me more," "Then what happened," and "Really!" The best time to do this reconnection is in the morning.

**Talk Less**. Acknowledge that you talk too much and cut back. If you have to speak, use one word, such as "lunchbox" instead of "you did it again, you left your lunchbox in the car. Go out there and bring it in," "backpack" instead of "I'm tired of tripping over your backpack, you know where it belongs so put it away now," or "teeth" instead of "it's almost time for bed and you have school in the morning. Go in there and brush your teeth."

**Set Up Agreements**. Getting your child to do something that you want her to do requires an agreement in advance. When she is in a good mood and open to discussion, request her time by asking, "Is now a good time to talk?" If she says no, come to an agreement on a specific day and time when the two of you can talk. If necessary, write it on the kitchen calendar. If your child says yes, get to her eye level and ask for what you want, and then ask her if she will agree to what you are asking. Be sure to narrow your request to a clearly specific task with a time and even a date if necessary. To complete the agreement, ask your child to restate what she agreed to and thank her for her time and cooperation. You will experience more success and find yourself talking less when setting up respectful agreements.

**Learn To Be More Calm and Peaceful**. When a parent is stressed over her work load, anxiety can be transmitted through an invisible connection to the child. As a result, the child may act out, misbehave, not listen, and mimic the parent's distress. Take time out to calm yourself and breathe. Simple meditation isn't just for those who practice Yoga. Becoming centered and calming your mind can have extraordinary impacts on your effectiveness as a parent. Your child will learn how to be more peaceful by the example you set for him in your daily life.

# The Cure for Parent Deafness

Sounds unusual, doesn't it? Getting them to do more by talking less? You might be thinking, if only it could be that easy. One of the biggest secrets for successful parenting comes from the animated TV classic, "Peanuts." The holiday versions were always my favorites when I was a child. The holidays weren't complete without being able to stay up to watch those special shows on television. However, I was always stumped over the teacher's muffled sounds in the classroom. She seemed to be making a sound like "Wah, wah, wah." Many years later while parenting one of my children and delivering a typical fatherly lecture, my oldest daughter made a remark one day that revealed to me she didn't hear a word I had said. I don't remember exactly what she had said to me but the gist was that she heard me say "Blah, blah, blah…" I remember at that moment feeling angry with her for implying that I had said nothing really important, or that she purposely did not hear me. Thinking about it after I had a chance to cool down caused me to hear the message she was actually trying to deliver, loud and clear. Sometime after that, I decided to stop lecturing my children and actually began to talk less often.

Talking too much to your children, especially through lecturing, reminding, reprimanding, scolding and criticizing can have detrimental effects on your power as a parent. It can cause your children to stop listening to you and go into what I call "Parent Deafness." When this happens, they begin to tune you out. More importantly, they may begin to listen more to others, such as their peers. Let me present this as the most important reason for you to talk less.

Parents mean well, especially moms. They have years of experience and wisdom they want to share with their children to help them grow strong and become effective adults, to live a full and happy life. An entertaining video comedy bit I've seen on this topic is a musical piece from comedienne Anita Renfroe, a segment she calls "Total Momsense." She takes every phrase or statement a mom makes in a 24-hour period and adapts it to the tune of the William Tell Overture. It's worth taking a look if you haven't seen it yet. Just Google "Momsense" or do a search on youtube.com to find it. While this video is funny, it reminds us all that we talk too much and cause our children to tune us out.

Instead of talking too much to your children, here are some suggestions to help keep your kids tuned in before you lose their attention.

**Stop Repeating Yourself**. Children are incredibly smart and know your rules and boundaries if you've taken the time to set them up correctly. However, they may do whatever they can to get you to break them if you've given in to their demands in the past. Stop repeating your rules, reminding them of what they already know. You can state the rule once and then let it go or better yet, ask them to state the rules for you.

**Set Up Agreements Ahead of Time**. Whenever you want your child to do something, sit down with him and have him help you come up with an agreement. Explain what you need and then ask for an agreement to follow through. Talk about what the task will look like when accomplished and negotiate the time required. An agreement is only complete when the child verbalizes the terms, not just when the parent states the rules. See other chapters for more help on agreements.

**Guide Them Respectfully To Follow Through**. This is another of my favorites. Once you have an agreement with a child, there is no need to say anything about it again until it has been completed and you are voicing thanks for her cooperation. But if you have discovered that the agreement was not fulfilled, go to the child and gently place your hand on her back and guide her to the location where the agreed-upon action was to take place. Do this with a friendly look and without speaking. Once you reach the location, walk away in silence. If she still doesn't complete the task, then you never had an agreement from the start. If it doesn't work the first few times, keep doing it anyway. I used this with all my children and grandchildren, and it worked. It takes time, practice, and your patience to make it work with children capable of creating agreements. The best part is that it may be even more effective with preteens and teens. Whenever I had set up an agreement with one of my teenage children and soon learned that he did not follow thru, I would seek them out with a friendly look and an outstretched arm, ready to place my hand on his back. I remember with a chuckle how he would much rather complete a chore than allow me to lovingly guide him to it. It still makes me laugh to recall my son's exclamation: "Dad... stay right where you are and don't come any closer! I'm going to do the chore right now!"

# Handling Power Struggles

Power struggles develop every day at work, at the store, and even jockeying for that spot in the parking lot. Just look around you the next time you're out driving; someone cuts you off, blocks you from entering a lane, or rides your bumper. Initiating a power struggle is a way of expressing the frustration of being overpowered by others, the feeling of having little or no power, or being ignored and forced into feeling insignificant. It makes us want to push back for our own power. The same goes for children. When they feel overpowered or insignificant, and want something from us (or know we want them to cooperate), they then initiate a power struggle.

As parents, our ultimate desire is to prevent all power struggles with our children. These confrontations are difficult to handle, strain relationships, and are just stress-producing. We can actually avoid power struggles with our children by willingly and regularly offering them more power. Appropriate power such as helping us around the house, including them in decision-making, asking for their opinion, and giving them tasks that make them feel important and valuable are things we can implement to reduce the struggles. Assigning chores to a child isn't always the answer, especially if they are presented as orders or if the tasks are too difficult. If the assignment doesn't produce feelings of power and importance, it will be ineffective.

Now that you know the real solution to avoiding power struggles, begin looking for opportunities to use it on a regular basis. You will notice immediate results through more cooperation from your child. When a power struggle does ignite, it may have been triggered either by something they want from you or something you want from them. The solutions for each are different and are explained below.

**What to Do When They Want Something from You**.  Here's a technique for situations when a child asks for something repeatedly until you cave in.  It might be a cookie right before mealtime, a toy while in the store, something they want to play with, or a place they want to go.  It's a favorite I've used for years with my children, from the preschool years into the teens.  When your child first asks for the item you don't want him to have, be firm and loving by stating, "I'm not willing for you to have that right now."  Avoid saying "No" because it might encourage him to try harder to make you say "Yes."  Using the term "willing" sets up a personal boundary and avoids defiance.  When he continues to ask, get down to his eye level, do not talk, rub his back gently to keep him calm (if he will allow you), and give him a comforting look that expresses sympathy for his desire that won't be met.  Continue these steps until his pleading stops.  The secret is your demonstration of greater strength by holding your ground longer than he can, and doing it without speaking or getting angry.  Children who throw fits to get what they want have been taught to do this by adults around them who have given in to their demands.  If he drops to the floor and goes into a meltdown, let it happen.  It indicates that you are winning, and he is simply using another technique to get you to crack.  If you can learn to do this on a regular basis, you will actually teach your child that you mean what you say.  He may throw more fits in the beginning as a way of expressing, "I don't like this new thing you're doing," but he will eventually learn to respect you for your boundaries.  The most valuable lesson he will learn from your actions is creating respectful boundaries with others.

**What to Do When You Need Their Cooperation**.  Solutions to blocking a power struggle when you want something from them are very different.  I suggest replacing commands or orders with clear and appropriate choices.  For example, instead of saying, "It's time to take your bath," give them a choice by saying, "Would you like mommy to give you your bath or grandma?"  I remember picking up my granddaughter from the day care center one day, and I could sense that she was overtired.  I knew she would not respond cooperatively to my request to get into her car seat, so I offered a choice. I said to her in a cheerful voice, "Would you like grandpa to put you in your seat or would you like to do it yourself?" Immediately she declared she would do it herself and strapped herself in. Giving your child choices makes her feel powerful and creates less need to struggle with you. And if backtalk occurs, ignore it. That's right, ignore it. Difficult to do at first — and something that was certainly not allowed in our homes as children — the correct approach with children who talk back is to let it go. It is just another technique that they have learned to get us to react and to win a conflict. When the parent learns to ignore it, the child stops using it because it is no longer effective. Children do things for the impact of the effects.

Finally, there may be times when you don't have the energy, stamina or time to use any of these techniques at the moment. I've been there, done that. Perhaps you are late for work, feeling embarrassed in a grocery store, or just too tired to think. The only solution to a power struggle if you don't have the strength to do anything that I've suggested here may be to stop talking and take your child to your destination. Be as gentle as possible and just concentrate on arriving. Because we sometimes say things we regret, talking less may be the only successful strategy at the moment!

# When a Toddler Hits

A common question raised at my parent workshops and in e-mails to my Web site involves the oldest child hitting the younger sibling. It is often worded as, "Our 2-year-old has changed quite a bit since we brought our new baby home a few months ago. He's been hitting us and having enormous meltdowns. We're afraid he's going to eventually hit his baby sister. What do we do?!"

**The Child Is Dethroned!** Chances are really good that the 2-year-old may be suffering from "dethronement." For the last 2 years he has been the center of the adults' attention and the apple of the parents' eyes. But now they've brought home another child and he's probably trying to let them know how he feels about this new addition to the family.

Authors and speakers use a particular scenario to help moms understand what dethronement might feel like. All the women in the workshop are asked to close their eyes for just a moment and make believe that their husband arrives home one day with another wife. She is younger and cuter than they are and he asks them to share their jewelry, kitchenware and other items with the new wife. This immediately evokes laughter and growling from the audience. The women are then asked what they would feel like doing to the new wife. As you can imagine, the responses are not very nice!

It's not much different for a toddler or preschooler, or even an older child, who is suddenly asked to share her parents with a new sibling. It's normal for her to experience a feeling of fear that there is only so much of mommy and/or daddy to go around, so I had better get all that I can before my sibling does. This can create many new behaviors in the first child, such as hitting, meltdowns, anger and revenge. Some children may even revert to babyhood to regain the attention they once had, with baby talk, wetting their pants, or even asking to wear a diaper.

**It's OK To Be Angry, But Not OK To Hit.** If your child begins hitting you, don't take it personally and simply see it as your child expressing anger toward you. She has not yet grasped the ability to communicate her emotions effectively, and quite frankly, many adults haven't mastered this either. Have you ever noticed how some adults may slam doors, place dishes on surfaces with greater force and walk with heavier footsteps than normal, all to let someone know how angry they are? A young child hitting a parent is her way of saying "I'm mad at you," or "I don't like how things are going right now!" The first step is to talk to the child and set up boundaries when she is not hitting. Get down to her eye level and remind her of the most recent hitting incident. Let her know that hitting is not OK. Help her to understand that if she feels anger and wants to hit, she has permission to hit an inanimate object such as a pillow. One mother I know took her 3-year-old on a special shopping trip just to buy a "hitting pillow". They brought the pillow home and decorated it together with a bulls-eye mark.

The next step is to role play with the child when she is in a great mood so that she will know what to do the next time she feels angry. The message you want to send is that it is OK to be mad but it is not OK to hit. If you have role-played this situation correctly, the next time your child acts out and advances to hit you, tell her that you can see she is furious but remind her that she is not allowed to hit you. Gently guide her to the hitting pillow or bring it to her and allow your child to take out her frustration out on the hitting object. It may take a few examples for her to get the message and learn a new behavior, so be patient and loving all the while.

**Helping The Child Find His Place.** Now that you have a plan to channel your child's emotions and resulting behaviors, here is your plan of action to truly heal your child from feeling dethroned. Find some creative tasks or new responsibilities for him to feel more like a big brother to the new baby. Find opportunities for special, unique responsibilities. This is similar to the solutions you read about in the power struggle chapter — to minimize power struggles, help children feel the power they crave.

Many years ago at a parenting workshop, I suggested to one young lady teaching her 3-year-old son to become the "Diaper Bag King." Within the first 6 months after bringing home the new baby, she noticed that his "meltdowns" of frustration began to grow and seemed to occur most often when she was busy getting the baby ready to go somewhere. Following my suggestion, she took him shopping alone one day and allowed him to buy his own diaper bag. She also stopped to have lunch with him at a fast-food place, primarily to get the paper crown that is given out to children. When she arrived home she explained to him that he would have a new job in the family and taught him how to pack the diaper bag with supplies for his baby sister. For the next several days she role-played the new routine with him once each day. They would pretend that it was time to go somewhere with the baby and she would call out loud for him to hear, "It's time for the diaper bag king." His instructions were to put on his shoes and coat, put on the crown, pack the diaper bag and then wait by the door. All week long, he dragged the bag around, begging to go somewhere with the paper crown on his head. When the day arrived for a real trip across town, she told me he exploded with excitement. From that point forward, he became more cooperative and the meltdowns stopped!

As you can see, the oldest child may demonstrate some uniquely challenging behaviors. This chapter addressed the younger child. The next chapter provides guidelines for the older first-born child.

# Four Steps for Un-Spoiling Your Child

If you're afraid that you have given in too much to your child and have created a spoiled "little monster," it's not too late to reverse the damage. Committing to a few simple steps that I've outlined here can help shape your child's behavior and make them a joy to be with again. But before we examine what to do, let's first define "spoiled."

**The First Eighteen Months.** According to experts like T. Berry Brazelton, M.D., children in the first year and half of life who cry to be picked up and held often are NOT spoiled. In his book *Touchpoints* (Persus Books, 1992), Dr. Brazelton points out that it is impossible to create a spoiled child during this time because the parent is suppose to attend to the child's needs. Adults however, can create an "anxious" child by being "anxious" or annoyed themselves around their children when they become fussy. He suggests that parents create frequent moments (10 – 15 minutes at a time) of putting the child down and letting the child cry. By returning frequently to pick the child up, the parent helps the child self-regulate by knowing the parent will return. And the most important aspect of each encounter with the child is to remain calm and peaceful. This demeanor will help the child develop more peacefulness for herself.

**Over the Next Sixteen and a Half Years.** Children and teenagers who demand things of the parent and throw fits may be considered spoiled, but they are actually reacting out of frustration to the adult's inconsistencies with limits. A child whose parents create consistent, firm and respectful boundaries for them are more likely to be more calm, cooperative, and content. So, "un-spoiling" a child means committing to new behaviors as a parent and better management of limitations for the child.

**How They See the World.** Young children don't understand many concepts of society that are second nature to adults, and many teens don't understand them if the adults around them are behaving badly. Some of these concepts include time management, commerce, supply & demand, and safety issues. And because adults are living very full lives, it is often hard for them to see the world through their child's eyes. For example, a child may throw a fit in the discount store because she doesn't understand why she can't have the toy off the shelf, especially if the adult allowed her to have toys off of shelves on other occasions. A nine year old may throw a fit because many of his friends have cell phones and he doesn't understand that his parents have decided to not "go with the flow" of other misguided parents and not let him have one so soon.

If you feel that you have spoiled your child by giving in too often, here are a few things you can do now to change that behavior:

**Own Your Part.** In their book *The Courage to be Imperfect* (Hawthorn Books, 1978), Turner and Pew wrote about the extensive work of psychiatrist Rudolf Dreikurs and how he changed families and marriages by teaching adults to own their part of a behavior situation. Dreikurs used to ask his patients, "Do you want to save the relationship or destroy it?" If you're willing to accept the fact that you may have created or contributed to the "spoiled" behavior of your child, jump start the transformation by acknowledging that you may have been inconsistent with limits and boundaries, and may have also managed your emotions poorly whenever the children were testing you or asking for what they wanted.

**Remain Calm.** When your child begins to ask for something, remain calm and say little. Acknowledge him for having the courage to ask for what he wants by saying, "What I love about you is that you know what you want and you aren't afraid to ask for it." He will need this skill when you aren't around and acknowledging it will strengthen it. Your disposition is also vital to teaching your child to handle their frustration and anxiety. The more unbalanced your emotions appear, the more unbalanced your child's emotion will become. You and your state of calmness is more powerful than you might realize and it will also set an example for your child to learn about self-control.

**Use Alternatives to the Word NO.** The response of "NO" from a parent, who has given in frequently to a child's previous demands, has little credibility with the child. Therefore the child is compelled to continue badgering the parent until the adult caves in to the request as they have done in the past. I suggest replacing the use of the word NO with, "I'm not willing." This response is far more effective because the adult is demonstrating full control over their own will. Keep in mind that you don't always have to have a reason for a decision you have made, and saying, "I'm not willing (to spend money on that)," or "I'm not ready (for you to do that)" is far more effective at setting limits. Be aware that your child may ask you, "When WILL you be willing (or ready)?" When they do, simply say, "I'm not sure, you'll just have to check back with me," and say it calmly.

**Set up Rules in Advance.** Take measures to think proactively more often and set up rules in advance. You know your children well enough to know what situations may trigger fits and tantrums. Before going into the store with your child or teen, get to his or her eye level and calmly go over the rules for the segment that is about to occur. Ask her to repeat the rules and then commit to not breaking them yourself, no matter what. Finally, acknowledge her for cooperating or supporting your rules when the shopping trip is complete. You will build greater success by concentrating only on what went well, rather than the failures.

# Nurturing the Oldest Child

The problem of dethronement can occur at any age. Take this question I received in an e-mail on my Web site. "The oldest of my three boys is 11 and he thinks that I don't love him as much as his younger brothers. He lies to me and bullies the younger ones. I'm afraid he's going to hurt them."

It all boils down to two things; dethronement and the tween years. Just as I described the symptoms of dethronement in the previous chapter, they can vary and surface at different ages. This 11-year-old may still be looking for his place in the family. On top of that, he is approaching adolescence and demonstrating a greater awareness of his self-worth. The combination of these two concepts can create new and different challenges that parents are not prepared to handle. Here is some perspective to help give you some understanding on what's going on and some suggestions for handling it.

**Characteristics of the Oldest Child**. First of all, what are the general characteristics of an oldest child in an adult? We either know one, grew up under one, or are one. When I ask this question at discipline workshops, I usual get responses such as "bossy, perfectionist, in charge, leader, responsible, etc." Whether you like it or not, your oldest child often has this internal sense of wanting a feeling of importance in relation to the rest of the children, and sometimes even wanting to be closer to the parents than the siblings. The oldest child likes to help mom and dad out and, to some extent, fulfill a need for leadership.

When parents have their first child, they shower them with attention, love and affection. When the second child comes along, the joy of having a baby in the house now draws the parents' attention to the new child in the family. This can cause the first-born to feel as if he has been "dethroned" and tossed aside. When this occurs, it is common to see a drastic change in the behavior of the oldest child. They can actually feel jealousy toward the other siblings and strike out to hurt them.

Take what we've discussed up to this point and now add the reality that this child is almost a teen and beginning to feel an ever-greater need to be important. The tween years (9 - 12) are a period of time when kids are preparing to separate themselves, not only from their siblings, but also from their parents. It's a time when they begin challenging the world around them to prepare for the individuality that will help them find their place in the world. It's also a time when their need to feel important and valuable can cause them to be influenced more by their peers rather than the adults, if those adults are treating them in ways that cause them to feel unimportant and unheard.

All the behaviors revealed in this question indicate that this 11-year-old may be unsure of his role and standing in the family. The best thing the mom can do is to find creative ways to allow him to feel different from his brothers and help him feel valuable to her as the oldest child. Unfortunately, most of us were not trained to raise children in this manner. We were taught to demand compliance from a child through control and punishment. The discipline I'm suggesting requires creativity, a willingness to listen more and talk less, and an ability to set up respectful boundaries and keeping them in place.

**Family Meetings**. I suggest that this mom begin holding family meetings with the boys once a week. It will promote a sense of importance among all the boys and will help them feel a greater sense of respect from the parent(s). The meetings should be held on the same night of the week, following the evening meal and after all chores related to the meal are completed. Everyone should be included and if there are small children, the meetings should be kept short in order to keep everyone's attention. Everyone should sit in a circle and it works best if it's not held around a table, but instead, form a circle with chairs or sit on the floor. The importance of this get-together is clear to the children if the door is not answered and the answering machine is set to pick up all calls. I suggest starting each session off with something encouraging and even fun, such as a prayer, a song that everyone can sing, or even just an "encouragement feast" — each person in the circle tells each person present one thing they love about them. After this opening, the meeting can be used to discuss family issues that have been collected throughout the week from everyone. It's also a good opportunity to talk about anything from sharing chores, disagreements, allowances, bedtimes, or family vacations. Once this meeting has been held a few times, the children can take turns as the facilitator. For best results, it should be emphasized that one person speaks at a time and everyone's input should be heard and considered.

**The Scribe**. Another way of getting the kids involved is to rotate the role of the scribe. who serves as the meeting secretary and simply takes the notes, recording what was decided and what was said. Preserved in a tin box in my closet is a folder of meeting minutes that were taken by my middle child throughout the years of our family meetings. The lists of rules and decisions are presented in perfect penmanship in red crayon on white-lined paper. These documents are more valuable to me than any historical parchment paper documents I could ever own.

# Guidelines on Chores

Parents have many questions about assigning children household chores. As children, some parents were assigned heavy chores, some were paid for them to be done, and others had no prescribed chores. When two adults come together as parents but were raised with differing points of view on chores, they may become confused and unable to agree, and the child suffers. Sometimes, I'm asked, "At what age should children be expected to start doing chores around the house?" Many parents want to begin teaching their children responsibility and are eager to get them started. They are also not sure what are age-appropriate chores for the different age groups?

Children should be expected to begin helping around the house whenever they are ready to do so. Regardless of the exact procedures used, parents should create an atmosphere in the family that encourages everyone to clean up after themselves and contribute to an organized home. Also remember to be gentle with your children's performance while they are learning and not focus too much on perfection. Children who are constantly corrected become discouraged and eventually give up. They many not say "No" to doing their chores but may express it in other ways through their actions.

**Preschoolers**. Children 3 to 5 should be introduced to the concept of helping with tasks, not taking on chores, based on the concept of being helpful and encouraging them to feel like important members of the family. But parents shouldn't expect them to take on consistent responsibilities. Preschoolers are still in a mode of discovery and experimentation for learning. Some suggested tasks for helping are: Pushing in chairs, washing the baby, and carrying the diaper bag. Be careful not to create schedules or routines with them. At first they may want to help to show they are big boys or girls, but can easily become frustrated or overwhelmed and give up. Go easy on them and be patient when they don't cooperate. At about age 6, children are usually ready to play a bigger role in the family by helping out with official chores. Start with smaller and easy-to-accomplish assignments; putting them on a visual chore chart will help develop routines and habits. Once new chores are mastered, use family meetings to add new ones gradually.

**Assigning Chores**. So what are the benefits children reap from doing chores? School-age children begin to develop an understanding of responsibility and teamwork when they take on appropriate tasks. They will also feel like valuable and respected members of the family. Success occurs depending on how well the parent explains and delegates the assignments. Here are some tips for making assignments to your child so they will accept them and take full responsibility.

- Assign chores to your child while at eye level, speaking in a calm, respectful tone. You'll have more success with little boys by holding their hands and looking them directly in the eyes.
- Do not give assignments when you are tired, stressed, or angry.
- Come from a position of "I Need Your Help," rather than a demand or command.
- Offer a list of choices. Allowing children to choose appropriate assignments helps them feel more powerful, creating greater cooperation.
- Use a family meeting to discuss and select them.

Chores for school-age and older children should be clearly defined so they know what is expected. Using charts to create routines and to track progress provides an excellent visual tool for teaching self-management. Here are some guidelines to consider:

- Avoid monetary rewards. Children should be taught to complete tasks for the sake of contributing to the family and not for the love of money.
- Chores should be simple to manage and monitor.
- Agreements should be made with the child that the assignment

will be completed as demonstrated. This involves a child's verbal agreement that the task will be completed in a specific way and by a specific day and time.

- Children should be taught self-management of their own performance rather than constant monitoring by parents.
- If a parent has to fulfill an assignment for a child who "forgot" to do it, the child should be encouraged to perform a task for the parent to make up for her mistake.
- Instead of reminding a child who has missed a deadline, lead them to the assignment without talking. Do this by placing your hand on the child's back and then leading them gently to the chore location or item. Then walk away.

Here is one final note on tasks not performed. A child who is sabotaging an agreement may be feeling a lack of respect or value in the parent/child relationship. Be sure that you have a full agreement from the child before the chore begins. If a child is not cooperating by failing to complete what has been agreed to, something else is going on. Some sabotaging also results when the child feels disconnected from the parent (or the family) because everyone is too busy, and it's his way of saying "No" to the assignment. You can have the best system in the world, but if the child isn't feeling loved, value and connected, it makes the chore system useless.

# The Power of Potty Words

Imagine this scene; little Johnny is playing in the sandbox at preschool and he hears another little boy say a "potty word". For the benefit of this discussion, I'll use a gentle one like "poo-poo." We've all heard our children use worse so there is no need for a reprise. Johnny repeats this new and unfamiliar word a few times because it's kind of cute and easy to say. There may even be a chance that he has heard Mommy or Daddy say it and he wants to be more like them, so he tries out the word. Moments later, the teacher is close by and hears little Johnny use this word. She's shocked and scolds him. As a result of her reaction, he quickly discovers that this word possesses some sort of magical power. Later, mommy arrives to pick him up. With anticipation and excitement, Johnny decides to try out the word again to see what affect it will have. She nearly drives off the road as she hears him announce it from his car seat behind her. Looking in her rearview mirror, she exclaims, "We don't use that word in this family!" and thinks to herself, "My child is out of control and he's only 4!" Or she's wondering, "What are they teaching them at this school?" Little Johnny is excited about the impact he has on the adults around him when he uses the word. If he could, I can imagine him saying to himself, "I'm going to save this powerful word for later… when Grandma comes over to visit!"

**Avoid Overreacting**. It's common for young children to hear various "potty words" and begin using them against our wishes. What motivates them is the reaction from their parents and other adults. Your child may be feeling small and unimportant, and suddenly discovers that using this special word gives him the power to cause you to over-react. Behavioral experts tell us that children may spend one to three months using a new word they've heard, but if using it causes mommy to lose her cool, the child may keep using it far beyond the normal "discovery" period. This gives him the feeling of power, and it even turns into an amusing game.

Immediately, I suggest avoiding over-reaction. This will take away much of the motivation for your child to keep using the word. Remain calm and avoid fearful thoughts that your child is bad, or worse, that you're a bad parent. Also, avoid punishment. Many of us can remember having our mouths washed out with soap or being punished in other ways. Instead, calmly and at their eye level, let your children know that you do not like the word and cannot allow anyone in the house to use it. Let them help you come up with an entertaining word that they can substitute. Because they may test you to see how "real" you are with this new boundary, be ready to calmly remind them of your rule about the word, and make it fun and exciting to use the alternate word instead. Taking this firm and loving approach will teach your child much more about unconditional love and building respectful boundaries with others.

**When it Becomes a Game.** Your child's use of a disapproved word can either be entertaining for them or a reflection of a power struggle. In the case of the game, play it down and avoid reacting. This only feeds into the fun. Your child might be saying to you, "I want to play with you," so look for alternatives. Occasionally, I would take my grandchildren on trips or shopping at the mall. When Aurora was about 4, she would love to play games with me by getting me to chase her. She discovered that at times I would be weighed down with diaper bags or suitcases and she would shout, "chase me grandpa, chase me!" and would then proceed to run away from me at airports or the mall. Yelling and getting angry didn't work because she didn't understand the danger of it and it only fed into her joy of the game. I quickly learned to do things differently: Go over the rules of the airport or the mall before entering, and at the same time, find much safer opportunities to play with her.

**When it's a Play for Power.** When the potty word is being used as an expression of power, once again, don't allow yourself to react emotionally. Simply state a rule about using the word. Recognize it as your child's demonstration of power, make a big deal out of finding an alternative word, and then redirect his attention by finding methods of expressing power. Go to the earlier chapter for more suggestions on power struggles.

# Handling Tragic News and Disasters

Preschoolers and young school-aged children easily can be frightened by images of disasters. They live in a world somewhere between reality and fantasy, and often have difficulty distinguishing between the two. They also have not yet developed their full understanding of mortality, or whether something on television is far away or close by. I helped parents with this issue following the Columbine school shooting in 1999, the World Trade Center attack in 2001, and immediately after the tsunami that hit Thailand in 2004. Here are some guidelines for handling children's exposure to devastating events in the news.

**Limit Their Exposure**. This is a good time to fall back on effectively managing their access to the television by limiting the amount of time they watch it. If you have to watch it yourself, get your children involved in another activity at that time. There are numerous university studies that confirm the high amount of violence on television and the effects on children. Some of these effects include desensitization to the pain and suffering of others, more fearfulness in general, and increased aggressiveness toward others.

**Explain It to Them**. If they do see the news report or hear about it from other sources, explain it to them clearly and honestly, and at their own development level so they will understand. Be ready to answer all their questions and encourage your children to verbalize their worries and concerns. Look for positive stories in the wake of the disaster. Most networks emphasize the gloom and doom of the event, but "human interest" stories often follow, emphasizing the best sides of human nature. Accounts of heroism, rescues of people or animals, and humanitarian efforts to help with food and other supplies tend to follow the initial disaster-oriented coverage. One story following the tsunami recounted a tourist's story of seeing an elephant saving children from the approaching waves.

**Watch for Unusual Behavior Changes**.  If you sense that children know about a disaster but are not talking, the best thing to do is to create safe and loving opportunities for them to express their feelings. You'll have better results by asking them open-ended questions for responses in their own words. Remain calm and don't force them to talk about it.  If an unusual behavior occurs such as bedwetting, hitting or sudden meltdowns, be patient and don't get upset. Feel free to talk with your pediatrician if necessary.

**Manage Your Own Emotions**. Even if you're doing a great job limiting the television, your children can still sense something's wrong if you are worried or your moods are being affected by the events taking place. You may need to talk with someone to ease your own fears about the disaster. If you're feeling sad and need to cry, take care of yourself by finding ways to get some solitude. Don't hesitate to lean on family and friends or seek professional counseling if necessary. It's one thing for a child to see something scary happening, but when their "all-powerful" parent is showing signs of distress, it can disturb them even more.

**Fall Back on Your Religious Faith**. Take comfort through regular prayer in your family meetings or attend special church services. You can bring attention to the victims of the tragedy and those who suffered by lighting candles to honor those who died in the disaster. If your children are old enough or you've taught them to handle candles safely, put a large candle in the center of the table to represent God or whatever life's greater power is for you. Each family member then takes a smaller unlit candle with a drip protector on it and dips it into the larger candle to be lit. Candles with the special drip protectors are usually called "candlelight service" candles and are widely available. This exercise also teaches unconditional love and will help children feel safe. By blowing out the flame of their candle to represent being frightened or not feeling good, re-lighting it repeatedly from another lit candle shows them that love is never-ending. They will also see that they can get that love from God's candle in the center of the table, from mom or dad's candle, or from each other.

**Create or Revisit Your Family Evacuation Plan.** Setting aside time to do this and including the children in the development process will help them feel safe. Children automatically see their parents as magical giants who have all the answers and know what to do. Putting evacuation plans in place in the event of an emergency will demonstrate this power you have and will set their minds and hearts at ease.

**Get Involved With an Organization.** Take part in community action to provide services and supplies to the victims of the disaster. You may find many local groups such as the American Red Cross or Habitat for Humanity International that seek volunteers for packaging and collecting supplies. Many of these efforts may allow children to participate. When your children see you giving to help others, it models the spirit of giving in their own way. It helps build the moral foundation you'll want them to have as they grow.

Your children are small creatures exploring and learning their world one step at a time. When something devastating happens in the world, they will undoubtedly have great difficulty in understanding the causes and impact. Be ready to comfort them and love them even more than usual. Be patient and be ready. You as their parent are the most important teacher they will ever have!

# Raising Kids Bully-Proof

Two young children are playing cooperatively for a while until something happens and one child slugs his playmate. At the sudden sound of screaming, the parent or teacher runs to the conflict. In a harsh tone, she demands that the aggressive child apologize and immediately comforts the hurt child. The aggressive child is reprimanded and/or banished to a corner to think about his actions.

This typical response by the adult is ineffective. Demanding an apology from a child does not teach the humble need to take responsibility for the impact of an action, nor does it heal the problem of bullying and intimidation. Instead, it's a response driven by emotions combined with a need to set things straight immediately. We see a child being bullied and it hooks into our own past experiences. We may feel sudden fear and pity for the victim and a feeling of anger toward the bully. The aggressive child may discover that he gets inappropriate attention when he is reprimanded or sent to a corner. This teaches that bad behavior can produce a feeling of greater power and more attention.

**First Comfort the Victim.** The next time you witness a similar situation involving younger children at play, your first response should be to comfort the victim without pity or drama. If possible, you should also include the aggressive child in comforting of the victim. Ask him to retrieve a cloth, a blanket, or even a drink of water if it's appropriate. Be sure to use a quiet, calm and respectful tone as you take control. Your immediate feelings may involve anger or frustration toward the aggressive child, but maintain control and stay calm. Once the drama has cooled and the victim is cared for, take the aggressive child aside and remind him calmly and respectfully about boundaries and acceptable behavior. This more peaceful response to the situation will provide an outstanding model and learning tool for both children.

**What is Bullying?** Bullying is any form of physical, emotional, or verbal mistreatment in which one holds an unequal power over another, purposely and repeatedly with the intent to hurt or humiliate. A bully can be one tough kid harassing someone who is different in some way. A bully's behavior can be as simple as name-calling or as serious as confrontation resulting in injury.

No child is ever exempt from being picked on by a bully at some point in his life, and neither are adults. In a recent study released by the American Medical Association, it was estimated that 3.2 million children are victims of bullying each year. Being able to defend oneself when attacked by a bully requires both courage and skill – traits you can begin instilling in your child at any age.

**Teach Them How Not To Be A Target.** A bully's common target is someone who demonstrates a lack of confidence and exhibits characteristics of weakness or insecurity. Therefore, teach your children to stand tall, use a full voice, look the other child directly in the eyes, and exhibit confidence when stating what they want. If your child does this, it will help to reduce the risk of being targeted. You can teach this to your child by modeling it yourself. The most effective way of teaching children a new behavior is to role-play with them. Allow them to see what the behavior looks like by modeling it for them, then allowing them to practice. A child who stands, acts with and speaks with confidence is less likely to become a target of a bully.

A bully-proof child must have the ability to ask for what she wants, especially when it comes to personal space and safety boundaries. Children must have the courage to say things like "leave me alone," "don't touch me," and use the command "Stop!" in a loud, firm voice.

Teach your children that they have the power to stop anyone from touching them, hurting them, or taking their things. One of the most effective actions you can teach your child is described in many self-defense and confidence courses. Stand tall and erect, and distribute weight evenly on both feet. Hold your head high, extend their hand straight out in front of them with their flat palm toward the other child, saying "STOP!" in a loud and strong voice. A bully halted in his or her tracks by a child drawing a clear, personal, physical or emotional boundary is more likely to walk away, often even respecting a child who had represented a potential victim.

And finally, if you suspect that your child has demonstrated signs of being a bully, it could mean that you are overpowering him and he is acting out a need to acquire more power elsewhere. Experts tell us that at the core of most bullying is the child's need to feel powerful over someone else. The solution is to provide more opportunities for your child to feel powerful in appropriate ways.

# Raising Bully-Proof "Terrific Twos"

If you're seeing your child get pushed around by other children, will he easily fall victim to bullies in the play yard? If your child is pushing and hitting, could she become the bully in later years? Experts agree that the traits children demonstrate during the "terrific two" period (18 months to 6 years) reveal characteristics the child could possess in adulthood. With simple techniques, adults have the power to change some of the social interaction characteristics they see in their children with during these formative years.

**Provide good examples.** When your child is exposed to conflict in relationships, be sure that she is also exposed to healthy, positive conflict resolution. The adults in a child's life are living, breathing models. It's okay for adults to have respectful disagreements with other adults in front of the children, just be sure they see the follow up discussion or the appropriate "make up" when a resolution has occurred.

**Limit electronics that contain violence.** Preschoolers are little sponges and "soak up" what's in their environment. Violence in cartoons, commercials, and video games are played out in preschoolers' play sessions. Provide positive electronics learning experiences instead. If an inappropriate scene comes on the television, take the time to explain what he just saw, and if necessary, turn it off.

**Set up rules in advance.** When your child is open to learning something new, talk to her about the rules of behavior, such as "hitting is not okay," or "I cannot let anyone hit in this house (or classroom)." Say this with a calm and firm tone of voice, not in a scolding manner. When you see examples of appropriate behavior from your child, let her know by making a big deal out of it. It is okay to be animated with a preschooler and to give her a little bit of praise in regard to her behavior.

**Avoid giving the bully attention.** When one child gets aggressive with another playmate, avoid charging in to scold the aggressive child. Instead, put your immediate attention on the victim and if possible, include the aggressive child in nurturing the hurt or crying child. Once the emotion clears up and everyone is calm, take the aggressive child aside and, at his eye level, remind him of the established rules about keeping hands to yourself. Make the encounter brief and then let it go. Avoid creating a lot of drama or guilt. If the aggressive child is punished, he may be motivated to show aggression again to get even or to get more inappropriate attention.

**Keep playtime with others brief.** During the phase of the "terrific two's," children are learning about social experiences. They don't automatically see a playmate as adults do, and their feelings toward the other child can change suddenly. Instances of hitting or being aggressive may be indications that the children need to be separated or they have had enough of each other for the day. Don't get angry or over react, just end the play time and reschedule it for another day.

**Build emotional intelligence.** Children who purposely hurt other children have under-developed emotional intelligence (the ability to know how someone might feel). Preschoolers do not yet have a developed emotional intelligence, so don't hesitate to begin helping them develop theirs. When you see preschoolers experiencing emotion (positive and negative), get to their eye level, look curious about their expression, and tell them what you see, such as, "You look sad." Or if a child approaches you with a problem like, "The kids won't let me play," say to the child, "It looks like you're sad that they won't let you play with them. What do you think you could do so they will let you play?"

**Help your child feel powerful.** It's easy to want to be efficient and try to get everything done exactly how you want it done. But in the process, we overpower our children. Children who feel overpowered also feel like they have no say in matters and are very likely to act out the need to be powerful over other children. Look for ways for your child to have and feel some sense of power in daily life and he will be less likely to overpower someone else.

**Help your child become capable.** According to a recent article on the American Psychological Association Web site, a child who lacks problem-solving skills is more likely to become a bully, a victim, or both. Avoid doing too much for your child and let her perform age-appropriate tasks as often as possible. If your child whines because he wants you to do it for him, don't rescue. The whining is a way of venting frustration and manipulating you. Let the whining and struggling occur without reacting, and be ready to provide encouragement with every small success.

# Not in Praise of Praise

I spoke at a conference for educators recently. Following my session on discipline, a couple of teachers of school-age children approached me with a question regarding the use of praise and how it relates to growing self-esteem. Through professional development, they explained how they had been taught that using praise with children on a regular basis will undoubtedly result in good behavior in the classroom, while contributing to the growth of a child's self-esteem. What I discussed with them over their lunch break would end up changing their methods in the classroom forever and changing the results they actually wanted. Cooperative behavior should be the goal, not "good" behavior, and it can be created with less praise and more encouragement! The same should be true for parents. Let me explain.

There is a big difference between praise and encouragement; because most of us were raised with praise, it comes naturally for us to use this approach with our children. Praise is an adult's judgment of a child or their behavior. Expressing praise, we might say, "That is beautiful!," "You are a good girl," "You make me so happy," "What a wonderful job you did!" The premise of praise involves an adult passing judgment on children and possibly motivating them to do more in order to get the praise, or even worse, in order to please the adult. This creates an external motivation. On the other hand, encouragement is new to us and may feel uncomfortable at first. It helps children create their own assessment of themselves or their behavior, with our guidance. To use encouragement, you might say, "What do you think?" "What is your favorite part of that picture?" "Tell me all about what you just did," or sometimes just remaining silent to let the child do more of the talking. This creates an internal motivation in a child to want to

r the simple act of doing something and enjoying it.
ny children draw to please the parents or for the
g encouragement sets the child up to do things for
.. simple enjoyment of the act itself, for the love and enjoyment of drawing and pleasing themselves.

**Use Encouragement Instead**. In my opinion, adults should be providing more encouragement to children. Encouragement is the essential ingredient for strengthening the inner core that will help a child grow strong spiritually, socially, and emotionally. Encouragement is the action an adult can take to help guide a child to look inside himself for an answer to a question, a solution to a problem they own, or a positive reinforcement of an existing strength or skill that may need further development. With more acts of encouragement, children will learn to listen to their inner voice to help guide them toward smart, healthy and safe decisions.

As an example, let's take a child who has just drawn a picture. What is the first thing she does? In most cases, she runs to a parent to show the picture for validation. The parent's natural reaction is to praise the child and let her know how wonderful the drawing is, and perhaps even suggest it be displayed on the refrigerator. Once the praise is received, the child will most likely want to go and create another picture. This can lead to the child's desire to continue creating drawings to win more praise and in many cases, to please the parent. On the other hand, encouragement guides the child to look inside herself for the genuine satisfaction of having created something wonderful. Encouragement requires the parent to help children determine what they like most about the picture, how they feel about the creation, and what they would like to do with it. The healthier goal is to help the child focus on the feelings they have about drawing or the act of the creation, not only the end result or what the parent thinks. We want our children to love art, to love creating things, and to enjoy learning or playing sports. We want them to do things for the love of doing it, not just the outcome. The bottom line is that more encouragement creates internal motivation and a sense of satisfaction and accomplishment.

**Praise Promotes Pleasing Others**. Praise creates external motivation and causes children to emphasize what others think and feel, rather than what they think or feel. Too much praise can guide them into unhealthy motivations – living for others or for the goal of pleasing others. Imagine what might happen to a child who is raised by a parent, externally motivated to make him or her happy. Then suddenly the parent dies or divorces the other parent. The child's source of motivation is severed and he may begin to struggle at working hard and successfully. It should matter less what we, the parents and teachers, think of what a child does or creates, and it should matter more what he thinks of himself. We learned praise from our parents and teachers. and then passed it on to our children. The adults in our lives did the best they could with what they knew at the time. Today we live in a different world that requires different techniques for discipline and a different approach to rearing children.

This concept of creating a greater internal focus for our children is a leading contributor to the development of strong, healthy self-esteem and it sharpens one's ability to hear a true, inner voice, something we sometimes call intuition. For those of faith, it's also considered the true voice of God. Less praise and more encouragement helps to strengthen an inner core that will guide children and help keep them safe – at home, at school, in the playground, at parties, on dates and especially when you aren't around.

# When a Child Says, "I Can't"

A child who constantly says "I can't" is either saying "Do it for me" or "I don't feel confident in myself," and each of these statements reveals a different reason and motivation. It creates worry for the parent or simply annoyance, but the child is reaching out to the parent to communicate a need. Often, it is hard to hear what is actually being stated. Let's examine each of these attempts to communicate.

**Manipulation.** First of all, the child who is saying "do if for me" usually says "I can't" as a form of manipulation and may even whine, throw a fit, or follow the parent around until a need is met. These children usually have a parent who does too much for them, things that they can and should do for themselves. Their parent dresses them, feeds them, does their homework or chores, solves their problems, and may even answer for them when someone speaks to them. They create and continue to support a child who learns to manipulate others to do things for them. I don't fault the child at all; he is only behaving in a way he was taught. Think about it for a moment — wouldn't it be great if we could get everyone around us to do everything for us? But even though these parents know what they are doing is wrong, they feel it's easier to just to do things themselves so they can get places quicker and have things done correctly.

To be a successful parent with this type of child, avoid focusing on efficiency rather than on effectiveness. Teaching and allowing our children to do things for themselves will raise them to be self-motivated and capable. Make the process of learning and teaching more important than the outcome. Be sure children know how to do something; then give them plenty of opportunities to do it themselves. If you ask them to put on their shoes and they throw a fit, when it comes time to leave simply carry them and their shoes to school. Don't get into arguments with them and be sure that you are giving them instructions in a respectful and loving tone of voice. Some children communicate the same way their parent does. If you've been doing too much for them and you've now decided to do less, be ready for them to be frustrated with your change. Be patient, give them space and be consistent.

**A Matter of Avoidance**. On the other hand, the child whose expressions of "I can't" mean "I don't feel confident in myself." This demonstrates a lack of belief their own capabilities. Their actions, words, and behaviors are not about manipulation but instead; express a genuine feeling that they lack competence. Physically, this child usually appears slumped over and he may even look down or close his eyes when speaking. These children express themselves in a quiet voice and do not usually throw a tantrum. If the parents of this child were to leave the room at a moment of an "I can't" expression, they would most likely come back a few moments later to find the child still there in the same position. Such children feel that they are incapable of doing some or most things successfully. They feel inadequate and may want to avoid the feeling of failure.

To be a successful parent, start by not allowing yourself to feel sorry for your child. This will only contribute to feelings of worthlessness, so it's important to avoid the "pity party." When you give them an instruction, get down to their eye level and speak to them with a positive and encouraging tone. When they respond with their weak "I can't do it," smile at them and say in an encouraging tone, "I know you can do it!" and then walk away. If you return and they still have not completed your request, move on without making anything of it. Whenever you do see them completing something on their own, make a big deal of it and acknowledge what they accomplished. These children need a great deal of encouragement and boosts of regular support. Set an example for them when you accomplish something yourself. Catch yourself doing something that might be amazing to them and demonstrate self-encouragement in front of them as a role model.

**Start With Self-Examination.** Being an effective parent means being able to solve your child's problematic behaviors before applying the appropriate discipline, and then knowing what action to take. To begin this detective process requires an understanding of your own feelings that erupt when your child's behavior becomes a problem for you. If your child falls into the first "I can't" example, you might find yourself feeling manipulated, annoyed and perhaps even angered. This may produce anger toward your child; you might snap at them unexpectedly, and decide to avoid the conflict by doing it yourself. If your child falls into the second example, you may first feel annoyance, followed by pity and a desire to perform a rescue. Sharpening your discipline skills by tuning into what you're feeling inside at the moment will lead you to a more effective response.

# Teaching Problem Solving Skills

Picture this scene: A child walks into the room and exclaims will full exasperation to the parent, "I'm bored!" After a few moments with no response, the child repeats the phrase a bit louder. (You may have never experienced this so you might have to imagine this scene.) I offer this scenario to the adults in my parenting class and ask, "Whose problem is it that the child is bored?" Amazingly, most answer confidently, "It's the child's problem." But when I ask the parents what they might say in response if their child made this statement, many reveal that they would offer their child options or suggestions for activities. This is inappropriate because the parent is solving the child's problem.

All problems have owners. When a parent takes over problems the child owns, the parent teaches the child that she is not capable; as a result, the child grows more needy and dependent on the adult. The child may even grow more demanding if the adult doesn't continue to do things for the child, thus providing immediate gratification. Not sure what it looks like? Just watch any episode of the TV show "Nanny 911". A four-year-old demands that his mother put on his socks so he can go out to play. The nanny coaches the mother to stop doing too much for her child so the mother tells the child he can do it himself. He then proceeds to throw a fit and falls on the floor in an uncontrollable rage. The mother can't stand the noise and commotion, so she gives in and puts the socks on for him.

In my parenting class, I take the participants through an exercise called "Guess Who Owns the Problem." The parents are presented with a list of simple situations and have to guess who owns each of the problems presented. This scenario causes the greatest challenge: The child throws a fit in the grocery store, whose problem is it? Conversation triggered by this question reveals that parents want to stop the tantrum because it may bring attention to them or it may disturb other customers. The bottom line is that the fit belongs to the child; in fact, some tantrums are thrown for the express purpose of forcing the parent to halt them.

**Every Problem Has One Owner.** Identifying and turning a problem over to the child can be a tough challenge for some parents. They want to make things better, take action so things will go smoothly, or fix things because it helps them feel wanted and valuable. But the sooner an adult stops solving a child's problems, the sooner the child learns to become accountable and more capable. In my class, I emphasize that we were each individually intended to carry only our own burdens. When we take on the burdens (problems) of another, it overwhelms us and weakens the individual who owns the problem.

One day, my son told me that he had to create a visual project for a book report and he couldn't think of anything to do. He was testing me to see if I would solve his problem for him. I told him that I was willing to help him come up with ideas, and that we would alternate offering these ideas as we built a list. He could then choose from the list to fulfill the assignment. But working with me to come up with ideas did not interest him and he fell flat on his bed, moaning while looking up at the ceiling. I knew that deciding what project to create seemed like exploring space at the moment, but it was his problem to solve. I walked away. A few hours later he came to show me with pride a poster he made to turn in as his project. The next time your children express frustration or emotion in response to a problem they own, I suggest you follow this simple, three-step response.

**Acknowledge the Frustration You See.** When your child approaches you with a problem she clearly owns, use your best parent-detective skills to determine the emotion she is feeling at the moment. Then tell her what you see by saying, "It looks like you're sad," or "It looks like you're disappointed." If the child walks up to you complaining about a sibling, your response could be, "You look like you're mad at your brother." If she presents a minor boo-boo to you or even one that you cannot see, simply say, "That looks like it might hurt." This simple step begins to help the child accept that the feelings she is experiencing are normal. For younger children, this step is crucial to help them learn to identify their feelings. Sometimes there is nothing you can say except to simply acknowledge the fact that they have the problem. If your child declares that he is bored, an appropriate response might be "Wow!" or "Really?" Make a commitment not to rescue your child from a natural opportunity to learn.

**Ask Them How They Might Solve Their Problem.** Sometimes all it takes is to coach them to solve their problems. Listen closely to determine what the root cause of their problem is and coach them toward their own solution. Don't do it for them. If the child is bored, ask him, "What do you think you could do so that you would feel busy?" If the problem is a minor boo-boo, ask her what she could do to make it feel better. If your child responds by saying "I don't know," you can reply, "Make believe you know." Inviting your child to use his imagination sometimes works wonders. If children get stuck here and are unable (or refuse) to generate any options on their own, don't cave in and solve it for them. You may say that you're not willing to solve the problem, walk away, or simply remain silent. Whatever option you choose, remain calm and don't get angry. If you have been a parent who has done too much for your children in the past, they may test your new boundaries or express their unhappiness to your change. My advice is to let them.

**Offer Your Assistance, Not Your Service.** Once they have come up with a solution to their problem, acknowledge that by saying "That's a great idea!" or "What a great job you did coming up with a solution!" Your job is then to offer your help and not do it for them. If they brought you a minor boo-boo to see and they come up with the solution of a bandage, offer to open the package but let them put it on. The more often you allow your child to solve his own problems, the more capable he will become. We must commit to helping our children develop their problem-solving skills so they will grow up to become capable and independent young people. We are not always going to be around to do it for them.

# Whining and Meltdowns

Whining and meltdowns are extremely difficult to tune out or stop. Handling other things while this type of behavior is going on can be a challenge. The first impulse of many parents is to stop it immediately by pleading, reprimanding, punishing, yelling, or even unintentionally whining back at the child. Sometimes our response is a meltdown of our own. We want so much to get the situation and our children under control quickly that it may intensify the child's behavior. But if our meltdown stops the behavior, it could eventually destroy the child's spirit and erode the parent/child relationship.

These intensely emotional expressions reflect protest and/or frustration that a child learns by example from others or through the results achieved by demonstrating the negative behavior. Admirable parents are those who have learned to accept this behavior simply for what it is and not allow it to affect them emotionally. A common scene depicts parents pleading with a whining child, then "losing their cool" by yelling, reprimanding or punishing, and sometimes even giving in to the child just to stop the behavior. Caving-in serves only to reinforce the behavior.

**Don't Shut It Down.** First and foremost, I strongly encourage parents not to shut down the whining and meltdowns by overpowering the child through yelling and punishment. Too often, this tactic could destroy the spirit that gives children the ability and power to react in a way that keeps them safe. In the book *Boundaries with Kids*, authors Dr. Henry Cloud and Dr. John Townsend (Zondervan Publishing House, 1998) define this expression of boundaries.

*"Being able to protest helps the child define herself, keep the good*

*in and the bad out, and develop the ability to take responsibility for her own treasures. Children need to learn to protest when they are in danger. A child being accosted by bullies on the playground must scream loudly or run for help. A child must also protest if her needs aren't being met... it may seem crazy to support your child's being able to protest. Yet children who do not have this ability to protest – the compliant types – often struggle later in life. Some grow up being dominated and manipulated by more aggressive bosses, spouses and friends. Unable to say no to the bad, they are taken advantage of."*

**Be Ready With a Plan**. Here are two important pro-active suggestions to help reduce whining and meltdowns: Setting limits in advance and teaching children to do things for themselves. As discussed in other chapters, setting up limits and boundaries in advance is necessary so children know what to expect and where your limits are. Many children's protests are brought on when they encounter an unexpected boundary. Because younger children live in the moment, it's very helpful to let them know what to expect before activities and changes begin. For example, before going into the grocery store, let them know what they can and cannot do or buy, and whether they will ride in the carriage or hold your hand. Giving them an assignment such as helping to locate a particular food item gives them something to focus on and may reduce the chances of boredom and frustration. Be sure to give these guidelines while speaking in a soft tone of voice and at their eye level. Spending an hour shopping is for adults, not for children!

**Avoid Doing Too Much For Them**. Avoid doing too much for your children – tasks they could and should be doing for themselves. If your child has grown accustomed to being helped putting on her socks, talking for her, or emptying her backpack after school, she may resort to whining to manipulate you into doing things for her. If you're guilty of something like this, announce to her (when the activity is not currently happening) that she is now responsible for the activity. Let's say that tomorrow you decide that she's ready and you find a moment to declare that she will now be responsible for putting on her socks by herself, but the next day she begins to whine instead putting them on. Immediately get down to her eye level and say in a calm, encouraging voice, "I know you can do it," and then walk away to give her the space to do it without you. Don't make the mistake of reacting to her whining or tantrum. Acknowledge the fit for what it is — an expression of frustration.

**Three Tips for Success**. There may be many times when you've done all the pro-active things possible and still face unexpected fits of whining and meltdowns. Here are some tips for success in reacting to them effectively.

- Let your children know that you can't understand them when they are whining. Tell them that you will listen to them when they can talk to you in a calm voice. Be sure you are always speaking in a calm tone and setting a good example to follow.
- Remove yourself from the situation without speaking (being sure they will be safe if left alone) or, if necessary, remove them as well. If you're shopping and a fit ensues, end the task and take them home immediately without speaking.
- Pay close attention to their physical needs at the moment. Children who are sick or over-tired need immediate remedies for physical situations, not useless discipline.

One final note on whining: Remain detached from the negative emotion. Experts say that if two pianos were in the same room and a key was pressed on one, the same chord on the other piano would begin to vibrate. That's exactly what happens when someone close to us responds with negative emotion. The same emotional chord in our heart also vibrates and causes us to react. To see whining for what it really is... frustration... requires the ability to stop that vibration in our own heart and detach from it.

# When Your Child Yells "No!" at You

Does this situation sound familiar to you? You ask your child to pick up the puzzle she left scattered in the middle of the living room and the response is a sharp "No"? You respond defensively and an argument or power struggle begins. Worse yet, it occurs when you're tired, stressed or angry, and you then set out to get even with your child for using that word (and possibly even a tone), and for defying your command. You make your children pay for what they said and for not complying.

The word "No!" is one of the first words our children learned to say as toddlers and guess where they learned it — from us. We said it to keep them safe, to get their attention, and to let them know our boundaries and limits. But when they repeat it back to us, it catches us off-guard and becomes difficult to hear in response to something we need them to do now.

**It Gives Them the Power They Crave**. Our children use the word because it gives them the power they saw in us when we used it. When they begin trying on new things, they want to explore and feel that same sense of power. Sometimes they use it when they want to feel powerful simply because they know using it will cause us to react. When our children feel the need for more power and value, but we're not giving them appropriate ways to meet those needs, they may behave in ways that they know will make us act out, simply to feel powerful on their own terms.

**It Will Keep Them Safe Later in Life**. It is my opinion that overpowering our children to stop saying "No" to us is very unhealthy. Children will need this internal power to say no to others later on in life when we are no longer around to keep them safe. The ability to stand tall and let others know when a boundary has been crossed or when we are not willing to give ourselves up to others, is an internal safety mechanism required for successful survival and to live a full and happy life. If we force our children to stop saying no to us, then we rob them of the ability to say it when they will need it most, such as on the playground so they're not attacked, on dates so they aren't taken advantage of, and in the care of other caregivers so they aren't abused. They will also need it later in life in adult relationships so that they aren't mistreated or disrespected.

If I can win your agreement about the truth of these statements, then the challenge becomes, how do we allow our children to say "No" and not give up our authority as a parent? Here are five methods to gain a child's cooperation.

**Don't Overreact When They Tell You No**. Overreacting gives your children inappropriate power and may anger you. If they refuse to comply, turn your original request into an entertaining activity in order to get it done. Race them to the bath or tell them you're going to pick up more puzzle pieces then they will. If you find yourself becoming angry, walk away and let it go, and use one of the following ideas next time to be more successful.

**Use Choices Instead of Commands**. Giving a child a choice rules out "no" as an automatic response. Instead of saying "Go get your pajamas on," say, "Would you like to wear your pink pajamas or the ones with little ducks on them?"

**List Choices of Chores for Older Children**. Instead of ordering your child to rake the leaves or take out the trash, create a list of 3 or 4 reasonable tasks that you could use help with, being sure that what you really want is on the list. Tell your child that you need his help and all he has to do is pick one or two things from the list. Be ready to remain calm in case he doesn't pick what you really wanted, so make sure that you're comfortable with all of the choices listed.

**Say "I'm Not Ready for You to do That."** Because she will repeat what you say, avoid using the word "no" yourself. If she asks to do something that might be dangerous or something you're not ready for her to do, say it. Tell her that you're "not ready for her to do that," instead of judging her age, size or abilities. It also avoids power struggles, labels and arguments; instead, it models respect.

**Say "I'm Not Willing To Do That."** Saying "No" to your child when he asks you to do something for him, such as take him to the park or buy him something, models a behavior that he will repeat. Replacing the word "No" with the statement above demonstrates a personal boundary and is not just a challenge for him to make you say "Yes."

If you must say the word "No," be sure to say it in a way that is calm and respectful. If you yell "No" at your child, he will repeat it in the same way. There is a wonderful poem in the book *Chicken Soup for the Woman's Soul* (1996; HCI Publishing). The poem "Angela's Word" by Barbara K. Bassett is a moving verse that describes the life of a woman who was trained as a child by her parents to never say no. She then found it extremely difficult to say it as an adult and because of this, gave up so much of herself to others. But then her life changed the day she "got permission to say NO... she became a person first, then a mother and a wife!"

# Homework Coaching Before School Begins

With the approach of the new school year, parents become overwhelmed or excited about preparing the children with new clothes and arming them with all the important supplies. When we were children, it seemed as if our parents did a great job teaching us that these things, along with some scolding to obey the teacher and the bus driver, were all we needed to prepare for school. But within a few weeks of the school semester today, we begin to feel quite frustrated when our children don't seem to want to take responsibility for their homework.

So why does this seem like a contemporary problem that did not exist when we were kids? Back then, we paid more attention to finishing our homework and school work because of the consequences that would follow if we didn't. More of us had moms who were home waiting for us when we got in from school to urge us to get started on it before playing, along with autocratic fathers who were ready to administer punishments if the work was left undone.

The parenting style in today's families tends to be less autocratic and more democratic, as it should. In addition, children are coming home to more single-parent homes or homes in which both parents work. This requires parents to know how to "coach" their children to take ownership of their homework, a skill few of us have. Children who do not take responsibility for their school assignments and homework feel powerless, as if someone else is in control. The parent reacts out of fear that it won't be completed and resorts to controlling the child and the homework. The result is a power struggle between parent and child; the relationship is strained and the child begins to despise school.

The answer to this problem is to help the child plan ahead

and take an active role in preparing for the homework, before the semester begins. Here are three tips for encouraging children to be self-motivated about homework one to two weeks prior to the start of the school semester:

**The Supplies**. Sit down with your child and help him come up with a list of supplies needed to complete his homework. You do have veto power as the parent and have final approval on what will be purchased and for how much. You'll also teach him about money and shopping by letting him carry the basket at the store, select the items (with your guidance), and even use a calculator while he shops to add up his purchases. Depending on his age, you may even want to give him the money and allow him to complete the transaction. Many office supply store chains have employees ready to serve, so why not allow your child to work directly with the salesperson while you tag along and say as little as possible.

**The Location**. Homework is often done at the dining room or kitchen table, or worse yet, in front of the television. These high-traffic, distracting locations are not conducive to concentration and learning. Allow your child to help you determine where the homework will be done daily and have her help you set up this special location. You want to be sure that the lighting is appropriate, seating is comfortable and visual stimulation is low. Don't be afraid to mark it officially with a banner or sign that reads, "The Homework Center." This designates the space as special, reserved for an important activity.

**The Schedule**. Allow your child to determine when homework will begin and for how long. Sometimes, allowing a 30-minute play or snack period before the homework allows her to wind down and get into the frame of mind for learning, especially for a "latchkey kid," home alone before you arrive. Let students help determine one type of activity during this pre-homework period and limit their choice of snacks. And to help them learn to manage themselves, work together to set up consequences if they do not keep to the established schedule. I encourage the use of a planner or calendar to begin teaching them about time management and task organization. It will allow them to keep a log of what they accomplished and how long it took.

Before you know it, your child will begin to feel in greater control of the process and you will see results from this approach. Remember to be a coach rather than an overbearing parent by checking in with them often and being available when needed. A good coach keeps others on task, focused, and is available to clear barriers that crop up along the way.

If you're reading this after the start of the school year, it's not too late to incorporate these steps. Developing a homework plan with your children will help keep them focused and more committed to taking responsibility. The more you allow participation in setting up the boundaries and rules about homework, the more likely children will to take responsibility for their work. Doing it before school begins is a way of treating our children with respect. Successful parenting and effective discipline begins before situations arise or before problematic behaviors develop.

# Encouraging Children to Read

At the conclusion of one of my parenting seminars in Memphis, Tenn., a parent asked me for the secrets to encourage more book-reading by her kids. I asked her what she was currently doing at home. She responded with a look of frustration and revealed that coaxing, reminding, and begging were not working. I then asked her two questions: Does she limit her child's access to electronic entertainment (TV. video games, DVDs, and the Internet) and do her children see her reading at home? Unfortunately for her and her children, she answered no to both questions, the two biggest secrets for encouraging young people to read for pleasure.

Most adults today remember life during our childhood. Television entertainment was limited and we played outside with siblings or friends for hours on end. And when those friends weren't around, we read books. Some of us read lots of books. I remember how excited I was when I was able to go to the library and pick out a new book to read. I found myself so caught up in the adventurous world of Nancy Drew and the Hardy Boys that I couldn't put the books down. This desire to read throughout my childhood, influenced by the books read to me by my mother, made it easier to complete academic requirements in high school and then in college.

**Put Limits on Electronic Entertainment**. Today's parents face two challenges that our parents did not: Making the effort to set limits on electronic entertainment for their children and managing their own time so they can be seen reading. The initiative to manage the electronic entertainment doesn't mean just the amount of time and the quality – it also includes physical access. Whenever I speak to parents in my workshops, I always encourage them to put computers, video games and televisions in areas other than the child's bedroom. I recommend placing them in well-traveled, family rooms where their use can be monitored and measured. Placing computers and televisions in the bedroom hinders parents' efforts by giving children instant access to what needs to be managed. It also allows this entertainment to subliminally become a big part of their daily lives. I'm always amused with the nonverbal communication that I see between couples when they hear me talk on this topic. As they look at each other, one parent gets the elbow jabs and stern glances from the other.

**Create Space for Reading.** A big objection I get from single moms is a reminder about the lack of space in their small apartments and homes. Without a playroom or den, they feel they have no other options but to place the devices in the bedrooms and away from the common living spaces. They want their children to be able to use them regularly and need the emotional space from the noise of the video games and movies just to keep their own sanity. I ask them to consider that they might want to give priority to more peace and quiet, and an uncluttered living room or dining room, than to their child's supervised access to electronic media. Having and enforcing a boundary that limits time with video entertainment will give a child more time to read.

Creating limits is a vital and necessary technique for parenting. It helps teach children about moderation, about balance and boundaries, issues that will become very important as they develop into reasonable, responsible adults. I sometimes fear that we are raising a generation of "instant gratification" children who throw more fits and tantrums to get what they want because they have learned that throwing the fit gets their needs met. In my parenting workshops, I help parents understand that when children throw a tantrum, they are not bad kids and often don't require discipline. Children throw tantrums because they are frustrated and feel they have no control. A child who throws tantrums on a regular basis to get what he wants has been conditioned to do that by the parent who gives in to the demands of the tantrum. And with parents feeling overwhelmed, stressed, over-worked, and alone as a single parent, sometimes it's just easier to give in to the child to stop the tantrum. But it is this "giving in" that teaches them to do it whenever they run into a parent's boundary.

**Set an Example for Them to Follow.** If you want your children to make reading a priority in their lives, make it a priority in yours. Set aside the time to read to them. For young children, make the time to read stories to them, and for older children, find items of interest in magazines and newspapers to share with them. A teenager will be more open to something printed in an article instead of listening intently to her parent's lecture or advice. Set aside some time in the evenings when all electronic media are turned off and everyone reads something. Specially designated, well-lit areas for each member of the family can be fun and motivating to use. Remember that setting an example for your children is the most powerful method for teaching them just about anything.

# Getting Them to Rise in the Morning

You made sure your daughter had an alarm clock, a loud one, you knock on her door multiple times, you play music in the house and make plenty of noise moving around in the morning, but nothing works. You even promised delicious breakfast foods. Finally you decide to begin giving verbal notice and warnings that it's time to get up, which turn into pleading and begging, which in turn morphs into demands and threats. Before you know it, you are at your wits' end, taking privileges away and punishing your daughter for not getting up sooner and now making you late for work. If any of this sounds familiar, here are some suggestions and solutions. Teaching children to wake up on their own begins with a good night's rest following established procedures and boundaries around bedtime. If your children are younger and you want to avoid the scenario a few years from now, set up a bedtime routine as soon as you can, and keep it. Creating smart routines with younger children early on creates healthier children with good habits later.

**Teaching Children to Get Themselves Up.** Many mothers have asked me, "What is a good age to begin teaching my children to wake themselves up with an alarm clock?" and my answer is always, "It depends." If the parent thinks her child is ready for responsibility and independence, then go for it. It's never too early to begin teaching self-reliance.

When my children were 7, 9, and 13, I made the decision that I was no longer willing to wake them up, and took them shopping for alarm clocks one Friday after dinner. I gave them each enough money to buy one and made the rule that I had final approval on their purchase before they proceeded to the check-out.

I required them to select clocks that had loud ringers and were equipped with battery backup (we were living in the South at that time and power failures were common). I didn't want my kids to have the excuse of an overnight power blackout.

Allowing the kids to select and purchase their own clocks was the first step in having them take ownership for getting themselves out of bed; the second step was to ensure that they knew how to use them. When I arrived home, I immediately called a family meeting. I announced that effective Monday morning, I was no longer responsible for waking up the children, and I provided a coaching session for the kids to be sure they knew how to operate and set their new clocks. Then I held a drill in which they all set their clocks to the accurate time, set their alarms to go off in five minutes, got into their beds, and shut off the alarms when they went off. Conducting this drill may seem silly, but it ensured that I had done my part as the parent in providing the resource and the training. The training I provide to my children is a very important component to daily discipline. This exercise also eliminated any excuses on Monday morning such as, "I don't know how to use it," or "it didn't work." The alarm clocks were set for Saturday and again for Sunday and each morning they woke up and turned them off. I felt assured that they were ready to wake themselves on Monday morning, and I can tell you that they all got on their respective buses on time and without issues!

**Bedrooms Are For Sleeping**. In addition to equipping your children with alarm clocks, it's equally important that you implement and reinforce a regular bedtime, establish a routine and sequence of events, and ensure that their bedroom is conducive to sleep. A child's bedroom is not the place for a television, video games, DVD players, or computers. A child is much more likely to fall asleep if the room is designed for rest and not for play.

A child's ability to arise in the morning with ease is directly related to the amount of sleep they get overnight. Some children have great difficulty getting to sleep because they can't calm their minds and relax. For this I recommend creating quiet time at least one hour before bedtime to begin reducing a child's energy level. This requires shutting down all electronic entertainment and limiting their stimulation to talking, drawing, reading, or better yet, silence.

If you've taken most measures that I've recommended here and your children still won't get themselves up in the morning, be sure that you're not doing too much for them. Sometimes not getting up is a way of pushing boundaries to force you to awaken them — another form of a power struggle. One mother I know used to awaken her children with snuggles, hugs and kisses. When she drew new boundaries and stopped that wake-up method, they ignored alarms, warnings, and threats because they wanted that closeness with their mother they had grown accustomed to. Her only solution was to re-create that closeness in other ways.

What about fears or not wanting to go to bed? Responding to a child's plea about monsters in the bedroom or just one more drink of water is frustrating for parents and is difficult to determine genuine sleep problems from normal stalling. See chapters later in this book that offer tips on each of these situations and more. If all else fails and you suspect that your child is having real difficulty getting to sleep, consult your pediatrician for help. And don't let your desire for control in the morning or your fear of being late to work rob your child of the self-responsibility that they need for development and growth. Take the time and make the effort to create order, routine and calmness at bedtime.

# Handling Disrespect

A disrespectful child probably tops the parental complaint lists I've collected over the years. When I hosted my radio show "Parent Talk" on Clear Channel back in the late '90's, nary a week went by without someone calling in to express the opinion that kids today have no respect for adults. But when I dug deeper into the parents' complaints about their child's displays of disrespect, I often found something different.

**When a Child Uses the Word Hate**. The child asks to go to a friend's house to play and his request is turned down. He begins pleading with his parent to let him go but when he realizes that he is not going to get his way, he angrily shouts, "I hate you!" Parents usually revealed to me that they then found themselves snapping with their own anger and began demanding that their child take back what was said and apologize.

We adults know how much this word can hurt because we sometimes save it for the clincher when we are being hurt by someone. Merriam-Webster defines it as "extreme dislike or antipathy: loathing." But when I talk to parents, my goal is to help them understand that our children don't understand this word as we do. The emotional intelligence of a child is so primitive that they think they either love us or hate us and there is nothing in between. I suggest that a parent who is confronted by a child using this word should let go of the meaning of the word and instead, help the child understand what he is feeling.

One day my preteen daughter told me that all her friends were going to the mall on Saturday without their parents. They were all going to shop for a gift for a friend's birthday and she wanted to go with them. My offer to accompany them so that she could go did not go over well, so I simply told her that I wasn't ready for her to go to the mall without an adult escort. She immediately became angry with me and shouted, "I hate your stupid rules!" Instead of getting angry, I calmly replied, "You sure are mad at me." She confirmed my observation and ran to her room to cry. My belief is that my child has every right to be angry at me when I draw a boundary or set a limit. They don't have to like my rules and I'm not their friend. I'm a parent responsible for drawing clear boundaries and equally responsible for doing it without becoming angry at them. This balance between love and discipline is not easy, but when a parent overreacts to the use of the word hate, the child is prone to use it more often because the parent has given it undue value.

**Disrespectful Backtalk.** The ultimate in disrespect for most parents is backtalk. In response to a parent's commands, drawn boundaries, or even administered punishment, children attempt to express their objections as the last word or they fire insults back at the parent. Some children do it because they've learned that if they keep chipping away at the parent's limit, they can get them to crack, change their mind or back down. But most children do it because it's the final straw; the child is angry with the parent for taking a stand, so they fire last words and insults to get the parent equally angry. It's not fun but it provides revenge. Though I'll be the first to agree that it's not easy, my suggestion for dealing with backtalk is simply to ignore it. Early in my experiences as a father, I learned that my children used backtalk to get me to react, but over a short period of time I had taught myself through self-discipline to remain calm and not react to the words they used. Instead of reacting, I ignored their words, held firm to my boundaries, and walked away. Amazingly, the backtalk began to subside and eventually stopped. I soon realized that allowing them to have the last words reduced our fights and arguments, and actually strengthened our relationships. I also discovered that I was teaching, by example, how to be peaceful and firm.

Hearing someone say something disrespectful hurts and can trigger a vengeful response. Learning to allow my kids to have the last words was never easy, but asking myself one simple question every time they did, helped: Do I want to be right or do I want to be close? I knew that wanting to be right was an immediate defensive reaction to an attack, but deep in my heart I knew that being closer to my child was more important than being right. And I'm glad I made these decisions when my children were small. Today I'm enjoying wonderful relationships with all three of them.

## Handling Interruptions When You Get On the Phone

There is something magical about the moment you get on the telephone, a visitor arrives, or you sit down for a moment to watch something on television — your children mysteriously emerge from the woodwork and want your attention. It seems as if you can't get just five minutes by yourself; the kids are knocking at your bedroom door, asking you questions, or complaining about a sibling.

The problem is attention; they need more of it and they don't like it when something or someone is competing for what belongs to them. In some respects, children have this sense that there is only so much of "you" to go around so they have to get all they can of your time and attention before someone else does. But as in all other parenting situations that require a plan, there are things you can do that are considered preventive steps for avoiding this problem, and things you can do that are fire fighting steps for when it flares up.

Let's start with preventive steps for avoiding the annoying, intrusive behaviors when you're on the phone. The obvious answer to a child wanting more attention is to give them more when you're not on the phone. But most parents I speak with tell me they are already giving their child plenty of attention.     Here are some preventive suggestions:

- Set up one-on-one parent/child dates on a regular basis and with each parent. Keep this time sacred and avoid postponing or cutting the time short.
- When spending alone time with a child, avoid answering the phone or the door. This demonstrates the importance of this time with them.

- Help children feel more important by giving them assigned tasks that belong to them, allowing them to help and feel like an important member of the family.
- Allow older children to assist you with caring for younger children. For example, allow an older child to help with a younger sibling by reading or singing to them or allowing them to help with the bath.

To begin teaching your child that she can't walk up to you and immediately gain your attention during a telephone call, here is a preventive technique that I used as a parent and teach in my parenting class using role-play. Wait for a time when you know your child is in a good mood and open to learning. Getting to her eye level, lay down a firm and respectful boundary by explaining to her you will not interrupt your telephone call to speak to her when she wants your attention. Help her understand that speaking on the telephone is important and you must give all your attention to the caller. Using a passionate tone of voice, tell her that you need her help each time the phone rings by going off to play with something special while you're busy on the phone, and until you hang up. Then, when the call has ended, you can give her attention again. Ask her to help you come up with an activity or a special toy she will play with when the phone rings or when she hears you speaking to someone on the phone. If you want to invest the time, money, and energy into this solution, you could even take her shopping and allow her to pick out a special toy that will only be played with when you are on a telephone call. Whatever you decide to do, your child needs to clearly understand what her role is when you get on the telephone.

Your child isn't the only one with special behavior instructions for the call. You must be prepared to maintain your new boundary with three specific behaviors: Do not make eye contact with her, do not respond to her by speaking, and demonstrate affection in some fashion that will help her feel loved. Notice that I do not intend that you ignore her, but to simply direct all your attention to the caller while connecting with her through your touch. This can include putting your arm around her, allowing her on your lap, stroking her hair, rubbing her back, or some simple contact such as placing your hand on her shoulder or arm. This sequence of actions sends the message to your child that your boundary is firm but you still love her anyway. The result will be that she feels loved and will eventually wander away, bored by waiting for her turn with your attention.

The next step is to engage her in role-play so she can see what your new boundary will look like. Explain to her that when you get on the telephone and she begins to speak to you, you will not look at or speak to her. Giving her this information in advance will prepare her for seeing it in action. Once you have prepared her with her special "telephone" activity, tell her that the two of you are going to play "make believe" with a telephone call. You may even engage a neighbor or friend to call you back so you can have a real call for practice. When the phone rings, get your child excited about her new role and begin the role-play. She will most likely be enthused over her new activity but may also approach you to get your attention or to test you. Maintain your three behaviors until the call has ended.

When my children were small and this process was new for them, they each tried to get me to break my concentration on the call in their own way. In the beginning, some of their behaviors were a genuine challenge. My middle daughter learned that I wasn't going to respond so she would pick up the extension telephone and join in on the conversation. My oldest daughter would find a way to engage the other two in mischief to see if it would get me off the phone. And my youngest, my son, would drive his small die-cast cars all over my body to distract me as I was talking.

Implementing these new behaviors require your patience and plenty of practice. I suggest doing one of these role-plays once every day until you get more comfortable with it. Be sure to give your child huge accolades when she goes to the activity and leaves you alone. From this activity and your strength in following through every time the phone rings, your child will learn to be more patient and she will also learn to recognize and respect the boundaries of others. She will also begin to learn how to implement her own personal boundaries. What I've described here is preventive discipline and requires putting your energy and creativity into setting up a learning model in advance. It is also done using preparation, fun, play and practice. The only fire fighting discipline that is required is to implement the action plan every time the phone rings. You can then take this model and implement it in other situations such as when visitors arrive, when you are speaking to the other parent, reading, or even watching television.

# Are We Raising an "I Want It Now" Generation?

While watching Saturday morning cartoons, your son beckons you to the television to see the latest popular toy he wants Santa to bring him for Christmas. You're in the grocery store and your child throws herself on the ground and suffers a sudden meltdown when you tell her she can't have the candy bar. As a stay-at-home mom you spend just about the entire day with the kids, yet they won't leave you alone for one minute, wanting more of your attention. Forget the X and Y generations, it seems as if today's child is part of the IG generation, "Instant Gratification!"

As children, we watched our parents work hard for what they provided for us. They also continually told us how our grandparents worked even harder, for even less. Because of the little we did receive, we valued and cherished it. Many of us had to work for what we received. I remember my parents being unable to buy me a bicycle when I outgrew the hand-me-down bike I had. I got myself a newspaper delivery route and was paid 25 cents per week, per customer, and saved every bit of it to buy myself a brand new 3-speed bicycle. Because I paid for it myself with what I saved, I remember taking great care of it for many years.

**Why This is a New Problem.** The amount of "stuff" we have available to us today that we can provide for our children is incomparable and it all costs less. We're able to buy things today that we could only dream of owning when we were small, and sometimes we buy it all because we often had to go without back then. Our loving hearts as parents want our children to have what we couldn't. But the conflict occurs when our children don't seem

to exhibit the gratitude for what we are providing to them, the same gratitude that we feel. We seem to forget that our children don't know what it was like to go without and to only dream.

So our kids kick and scream; we cave in and buy it for them. Thus, they learn the unhealthy model that "kicking and screaming gets me what I want." Sometimes we are able to hold to our boundaries and not buy it all for them, but then our children see their friends getting the cool things. They then return to the "kick and scream" model we taught them and give that a try. When confronted with this negative behavior, some parents figure it's just easier to give in and buy it for them to stop the behavior. They either don't know what else to do or don't feel that they have the stamina to do what they know is right.

When my daughters each grew into their teen years, they automatically received the privilege of driving the well-worn extra family car that we had kept around specifically for this purpose. It survived the many years with the two girls driving it and each of the dents, scrapes, and bruises were earned in incidents which helped them learn from their mistakes. When my son became eligible to drive, his sister was still using the car. With only 2 years between them, she was still in high school. This got him somewhat excited because he assumed I would have to go out and get him another vehicle. Unfortunately for him, I came up with a new house rule: I was not willing to buy him a car but would match him dollar for dollar to help him buy his own. What made this rule difficult for him to swallow was that the neighbors on both sides of our house each went out and bought their sons (same age as mine) pre-owned sports cars. He whined and complained about my rules being unfair, and even hollered, "I wish I lived in their family!" a few times. I didn't blame him. When he protested, I let him. But within a year, he had saved up $400 from his part-time weekend job and together we went out and found a 10-year-old car that needed quite a bit of work. Its dents indicated that it may have been another family's extra car. I told my son they added character to it. He told me they were embarrassing. I can tell you that he took great pride in that car and worked hard to take good care of it. Every time he was out in the driveway polishing his car, I saw myself polishing that new bicycle as a teenager. Today he appreciates and takes care of everything he buys for himself.

**Stop Buying Them So Much**. Resist the urge to buy everything for your children. Just because you can afford it or because it's on sale doesn't mean you should make the purchase. Too much stuff creates chaos and a desire for more stuff. Recently, when my stepdaughter came home from playing at a friends house, she revealed that the little girl had a 42" plasma screen on the wall of her bedroom. She wanted to know why she couldn't have one too. Our simple response to her was that we were not willing to buy one and electronics are not allowed in bedrooms. Sometimes I don't even provide a reason for some requests, all I say is that I'm not willing to buy it. As a parent, I retain the right to be unwilling to do some things. Some children are not happy with any reason you give them, so why waste your time and energy? They just want to argue with you so that you will change your mind.

**Teach Them to Create a Dream Book**. Children should have the right to ask for what they want and to be able to do it without punishment. They will need this ability whether they are in danger or reaching for their dreams. The power to ask for things liberates them to ask for help, to shout "help me," or to urge a predator to stop approaching or touching them. Stifling a child's ability to ask for what he wants could compromise his ability to ask for what he wants to keep himself safe when danger may be lurking. Unfortunately, many parents rob their child's ability to ask for what they want because they become frustrated with the child's constant requests, and snap at them to stop. If you have a child who constantly asks for things, provide her with a composition book or notebook to record all the things she asks for. Allow her to shop for it with you and then decorate it to make it her special book. This could be called a "Dream Book" where she can draw pictures or record entries whenever she thinks of something she wants or desires. Whenever she says, "Mommy, I want you to buy me that new toy," her mom could say, "I'm not willing to buy that for you. Why don't you put it into your dream book?" This will help her channel her wishes and help you manage the constant annoying requests. You want your children to feel confident asking for what they want, whether they get it or not. It's simply OK to ask. Confident requests today for toys, treats, or experiences as a child will result in confident requests for jobs, relationships, and boundaries as an adult, enabling them to live their dreams.

**Create and Maintain Clear Boundaries**. Finally, go back and read previous chapters on teaching with boundaries. Setting up crisp and clear boundaries and keeping them in place with consistency will minimize the tantrums when they express their desire for things and test your limits.

# Exposing Them to Nature

I receive e-mails, letters, and phone calls with a wide variety of questions about children's behavior from frustrated parents around the country. When I read the question below, my initial reaction was to dismiss it and go on to the next, but a second reading revealed some powerful opportunities for these parents to teach, coach and guide.

*"Our preschool daughters caught a lizard in the backyard and my husband told them they could keep it in a jar. I told them it was nature and they had to let it go. They both threw a tantrum and a meltdown ensued."*

Aside from the fact that they were not working together as a mutually supportive team and setting an example for the children, the parents were also too focused on the lizard as an object. Instead, they could have used the capture of this lizard as an opportunity to teach the girls a little bit about our respect for nature, our partnership with the world around us, and an appreciation for different forms of life.

Instead of letting your children just keep a creature in a jar or demanding that they let it go right away, use it as a wonderful opportunity to examine the world around them and help them begin to construct their opinions and feelings about nature. There is so much to show and teach your children about this remarkable world in which we live. Match it with the powerful sense of wonder in your children's mind and you'll allow them to get away from the computer, the television, and the DVDs long enough to learn more. You might actually have some memorable together-time moments that will build your relationship with your child.

To the mom asking this question, I suggest she allow them to keep it very briefly and then let it go. While holding it in a glass jar to be examined, take some digital pictures of it and allow the children to decide which ones are their favorites to keep. I had a brush with nature last year when a raccoon showed up at my back door one evening. I ran into this overly friendly little guy while bring cat food out to feed a lonely stray, and he didn't seem to want to leave. I grabbed my digital camera and snapped a few pictures that became keepsakes to share with my grandchildren over and over.

Take the kids to the local library and research just exactly what the lizard is, what it eats, and the most favorable conditions for its habitat. Allow the children to decide where they'll let the little creature go, and allow them to participate in the release as much as possible. It might be a great excuse for getting out to your local state park to walk and examine more nature. Before you leave for the park though, see if your local state park has a Web site with a schedule of planned activities. During the warmer months, many parks have activities set up, allowing our children to connect with nature. You'll find nature walks, demonstrations, re-enactments, guided tours, and arts and craft events, just to name a few.

Once the little creature is released, it doesn't mean he's gone and the experience is over. Instead, the creativity can now begin. Go back to those digital photos you saved and pull them into an art or photo computer program to modify. You can blow them up, print them out, or modify them with special effects to create some wonderful art projects. There are special programs for children that will allow for importing photos so the kids can color them or decorate them. If you don't have software that will allow you to do that, pull the pictures up on the screen and allow your children to draw and color their own free-hand versions of pictures of the creature to name and share with family.

At this point, the little lizard is physically gone, but the experience can remain so your children can explore their own imagination and creativity just waiting to be released and experienced. Capturing a little piece of live nature temporarily to touch and see can be so enriching for our kids if we learn to coach them properly. It's also a great opportunity to shut off that electronic noise for a while and allow them to open their eyes to the true beauty around them.

# Teaching Children Gratitude

It's definitely a different world from the one we experienced as children. We work harder today to create comfortable lives for our families and it's hard to accept that our children don't seem to appreciate what they have and what we do. In so many ways it's become a world of instant gratification with just about everything available 24-7 for our convenience. But it's up to us to teach our children gratitude through the example we set and the discipline we use at home. Some parents think that discipline simply involves actions you take when your children misbehave and act out. It's not! As a variation of the word "disciple," which means to teach or to train, discipline means "the training expected to produce a specific character or pattern of behavior, especially training that produces moral or mental improvement," and it's an opportunity we have every time we are with our children. Parents need to spend more time and effort coaching, guiding and teaching, rather than just policing and controlling. Here are some ideas that will help teach your children gratitude.

**Teaching Them to Say It**. The phrase "Thank You" seems to lose its value when used too often or when it's hard to embrace being thankful; so how about changing the word to bring it more into your child's consciousness. Create some opportunity to enjoy diversity by teaching your child how to say thank you in a different language. My grandparents came to this country as immigrant children from Poland. They taught me to say thank you in their native language as Dziekuje (approximate pronunciation JE • KOO • YUH). I found an Internet Web site that has the expression thank you translated in over 465 languages: http://www.elite.net/~runner/jennifers/thankyou.htm. Similar sites can be located through your Internet search engine (such as Google or Yahoo).

**Helping Them to Visualize It**. Regular meetings are an integral part of generating a strong family. This get-together held a few times a month helps develop the family as a loving team. One possible activity in a family meeting is to have each person draw pictures of the things for which they are most thankful. The pictures could then be posted on the wall or on bedroom doors. One father I know even drew pictures of what he was most thankful for — his children. This helped his kids understand that he was grateful for more than just material objects.

**Show Them What It Looks Like**. I can't help but return to one of the most important methods for teaching our children: Setting an example. We have every day with our children to teach them to express gratitude by thanking them ourselves for what they do. Acknowledging their acts of service or follow-through on agreements and responsibilities sets them up for success and creates habits they will internalize from us. And for those of us who desire to raise our children with spiritual or religious traditions, thanking God in regular prayer for all that we've been given sets an example of humility, an appreciation of a power greater than we are, and for life itself. At the very least, say "thank you" to others in front of your children. Say it often and mean it!

**Teach Them How To Write It**. A tradition that seems to be missing from today's business world, the community and the family, is the thank-you note. I'm not referring to text messages, e-mails or greeting cards, just the good old-fashioned written words of thanks. I make it a priority as often as I can to write thank you notes to those who helped me accomplish my goals throughout the past week. I encourage you to seek opportunities to leave thank-you notes in your child's lunch bag or backpack, thanking them for what they did to help you or simply just for being here.

**Teach It Through Active Giving**. Teaching a child to be truly thankful can be taught most effectively by first teaching them to give to others, especially during the holiday season. Consider encouraging your children to cull out some of their clothing or toys. Find a local charity that accepts donations and allow your child to participate in the process to determine what will be donated, including going along on the trip to make the actual drop-off of the items. It's always much easier for us to get it done, but allowing them to participate creates invaluable learning opportunities. Allow your children to create things with their hands and bring them to others who need some cheering up. If your children are older, volunteer at a local soup kitchen during the Thanksgiving or Christmas holiday. Set up a process for your child to break up money they receive from chores or holidays into separate containers or envelopes for saving, spending and donating.

**Teach Them About the Thanksgiving Holiday.** Finally, teach them all about the history and traditions that led to the creation of Thanksgiving Day. Using family meetings, books, pictures, web sites and movies to help them understand the origin of the holiday will give them the foundation they will need for their future. Remember, our children are living representatives that we send to a time we will not see!

# Consequences vs. Punishment

Punishment can be an automatic response to misbehavior from parents who were punished themselves as children. But it doesn't change behavior permanently if there is no guarantee that the punishment will always be there. Punishment is neither kind, respectful, nor a form of discipline that demonstrates unconditional love. When a child misbehaves, a common response from the parent is to punish the child and make her pay for what she did. This is a response motivated by fear and/or anger, and produces negative feelings in the child. She learns to stop misbehavior out of fear (or even pain) of the punishment rather than from learning right from wrong.

Positive alternatives to punishment, such as consequences, may be difficult to learn and apply. But they permanently change a behavior through teaching and constructing a child's moral compass. The only thing that punishment accomplishes is to provide temporary relief to a caregiver from the stress caused by the negative impacts of someone else's behavior or actions.

One effective and healthier form of discipline is the consequence — a predetermined (logical or natural) action that will occur in response to a child's choice of action or behavior. Creating and implementing consequences is one of the most challenging items in a parent's discipline toolbox because of the lack of knowledge of how and when to use it. They are necessary and effective when a child misbehaves, creating a problem for themselves or someone else. There are two types of consequences: Natural and logical.

**Natural Consequences**. A natural consequence is the direct result of a child's behavior that provides a learning experience for the child if the parent does not intervene. For example, a child who forgets his lunch on the counter at home has nothing to eat at school and may go hungry for the rest of the day. After a few of these incidents, the child learns to remember to take his lunch to school. This created a teachable moment for the child. Coaching by the parent in advance to help prepare a child to take personal responsibility is helpful and positive, but intervening to rescue or scold the child is not. Parents who intervene and run the child's lunch to them at school rob him of the learning opportunity to remember it next time. This produces a child who forgets but has a parent who remembers for him.

Here are examples in which a parent should avoid intervention and allow the natural consequence to do the work more effectively: The child –

- can't decide if he wants to play basketball this season
- received a D on her report card
- friends wouldn't let him play because he was bossy
- is bored
- did not plan enough time to work on her book report
- does not like how the book report turned out

With problems such as these, a parent's involvement can focus on coaching the child to help him understand what caused the problem as well as helping him develop his own solutions for the situation at hand or to prepare for future incidents. The parent should also refrain from reprimands such as, "See what happens when you don't do your homework." Friendly dialogue between the parent and child is necessary so that the child will feel encouraged to problem-solve himself.

**Logical Consequences.** There are many occasions when the results of children's actions don't bother them and this can create problems for the child or the adult. In such cases, a natural consequence cannot be used and a logical consequence may be required; a predetermined action that will occur as a result of the behavior. The first step in setting up a logical consequence is to sit down with the child and create an agreement in advance about rules, behaviors, limits and boundaries. Once the child commits willingly to the agreement, a consequence can be created jointly by the adult and the child.  This consequence can even be documented and signed by both the adult and the child, and posted as a visual reminder.  When these measures are taken, children are less likely to repeat the misbehavior.  If they do, they are more likely to be ready for, and follow through with, the consequence.

An effective logical consequence must meet certain criteria.  Whatever is selected must be reasonable, related to the misbehavior, and it must teach the child responsibility for her actions.  It must also not contain any form of punishment.  Here is an example of the proper application of a consequence:  A family rule was created in advance to allow each child one hour of recreational electronics time on school days and two hours on weekends and holidays.  This included watching television, using the computer for non-learning purposes, and playing with the video game system.  A timer was used and each child was given the responsibility of tracking his own time.  If the parent noticed that the child exceeded their time for the day, he received no electronic time the following day.  So let's test the criteria for the consequence: It's related to the infraction, it's a reasonable action, it teaches the child about being responsible for agreements regarding electronics, and it could not be considered as punishment.

When my grandson was a preschooler, he loved to play with the plastic bucket filled with die-cast cars I had collected over the years.  Tiring of his failure to pick them up when he had finished playing with them, I decided it was time to set up a mutual agreement and a consequence.  I got down to his eye level and using a calm and loving voice, I announced that Grandpa had a new rule about the toy cars.  I told him that whenever he wanted to play with the cars, he had to agree to pick them up when he was finished.  He agreed to the new rule by repeating it aloud; then I hugged and thanked him for being so helpful to me.    Let me emphasize that you only have an agreement with children when they verbally repeat the rule.  Then, I created a consequence — if he did not comply with the rule, he would lose the privilege of playing with them next time.  After three incidents of losing the privilege and throwing a fit when I implemented the logical consequence, he learned to pick up his toys when he finished playing with them.

One final note on logical consequences involves the delivery.  A logical consequence must be implemented without a trace of anger because it is designed to teach them about cooperation, responsibility and limits. In order to work, a logical consequence must be delivered with respect and love in your voice, your face and your actions.

# Eating and Mealtime

I was invited to speak at the Arkansas State Conference on Kids and Nutrition one year; my talk was based on winning the battles over getting kids to eat and getting them to eat well. The majority of the questions I received seemed to center around restaurants, getting them to remain seated during mealtime, and holidays.

**Kids and Restaurants.** First and foremost, restaurants were not made for children, they were made for adults. If you still want to pursue the dream of a delightful dining-out experience, the next thing I suggest is to do three things. Eat at a family-friendly restaurant that caters to children, bring a bag of activities to keep them busy and focused, and then make a big deal of it whenever they are behaving appropriately. If nothing here works, then get a sitter and eat out alone occasionally as a couple. My granddaughter, like her mother, has always been a challenge at restaurants. She talks loudly, gets up and down from her chair constantly, picks fights with her brother, throws her menu on the floor to see what will happen, talks to everyone around our table, and constantly shouts to the wait staff walking by, "Excuse me, do you have any crayons? I don't have enough colors!" I've learned to either tolerate it, get her engaged in activities like counting the different colored sugar packets, or eat at a fast-food chain restaurant.

**Getting Kids to Cooperate At Mealtime.** The common complaint is getting the kids to eat what has been prepared. Sometimes children won't eat what you want them to eat as an extension of the power struggle. They feel over-powered, bossed around, and simply small during the majority of the day, and then discover that you want something from them at mealtime. Others just resist trying something new, and may have real dislikes for tasting or eating certain foods. Cooperation may also be minimal when they are tired and hungry at mealtime. I suggest parents prepare a common alternative to whatever is being served at the meal and allow their children to select the main menu or the old standby. When my kids were little, our backup was a cup of dry Cheerios. In other words, the kids could pick from having what Mom or Dad fixed for the meal, or they could pick the cup of Cheerios. In the beginning, for some of our children, the alternative was the immediate selection. As most parents do, I worried about proper nutrition if all they ever ate for dinner was cereal. But being consistent with our rules and boundaries, the Cheerios soon grew old and we found the children more willing to eat the prepared, hot food. Then, as they grew, we added a few more alternatives such as crackers and eventually, a peanut butter and jelly sandwich. We never allowed anything sweet as an alternative, such as sugared cereal or cookies, and the PB&J wasn't allowed until they were teens. The object of the alternative is to give them a choice at mealtime and make it something very simple that does not require additional preparation.

**Handling Holiday Meals**. What do you do if they won't behave during the holiday meal? I've heard some parents express the view that if their kids could just be cooperative for one or two special meals a year, it would have to be during the holidays. We dress them in their special outfits, invite the relatives we rarely see, and just want everything to be right. But then the kids won't sit still, they mess up their clothes, or worse yet, say or do astonishing things that end up embarrassing us. We have in our mind how the kids should behave and it's usually based on how we behaved when we were children. But the problem is that raising kids was much different then. It was a much simpler world with less stimulation, no video games, and highly controlled entertainment. Our parents used more autocratic parenting methods and held the family to stronger, greater traditions and routines. We behaved differently, that's a fact. So one of worst disappointments comes when we compare our childhood to the image we want for our children. Parents will experience much more joy and happiness around the holidays if they relax more and reduce their expectations for creating the memories of get-togethers in the distant past. Besides, we make up or embellish so many of our memories, especially about holiday gatherings long ago. We re-create a fondly remembered, nostalgic glow and create an unrealistic expectation, setting the bar too high for today's world. With relatives arriving who will give more attention to the children and magical events that only happen during this time of year, the excitement can be so great for our children during the holidays that it is bound to change behaviors.     One more thing about kids and eating is to keep their portions small.  Overloading a child's plate with food can be so overwhelming to them.  Try putting very small amounts of all the items prepared for the meal on their plate.  You may find them suddenly asking for more.

# Help! My Child Visited an Adult Web Site!

I received an e-mail from parents seeking help in monitoring their child's use of the Internet. They had only a suspicion that their son visited an inappropriate Web site and wanted to know how long they should ground him from using the computer. My response to the parent was that they had more work to do than just the grounding.

As mentioned previously, parents should be actively using two approaches: preventive and fire fighting. Preventive parenting consists of all the things parents should be doing all the time, especially when the children are behaving well. Fire fighting parenting involves the immediate actions that must be taken when misbehavior occurs. The more time and attention given to preventive parenting practices, the less likely or less often misbehavior erupts, minimizing the need for fire fighting responses.

If you suddenly discover that your child has used the Internet inappropriately, the following immediate fire fighting action plan will help. Then, you'll find some preventive parenting suggestions to keep this from occurring.

**An Immediate Action Plan**. At a time when you can remain calm, in full control of your emotions and actions, ask your child respectfully for his time: "Is this a good time to talk with you?" If he responds negatively, ask him for a better time and set up an appointment. Be sure to follow through and be available for him at the predetermined time and place. This technique may sound silly if you've never used it before, but it demonstrates respect for him and his time. When we demonstrate respect for our children, their space, thoughts, ideas and time, it creates a model that encourages them to feel respected by us and be more cooperative. When the discussion finally occurs, begin by getting to his eye level. This, in itself, also makes the child feel respected and valued, and more likely to respect you in return. Next, relay the information that you are aware that someone was on an inappropriate Web site and you are not pleased about it. You want to be very clear that you are in charge of the use of your (or the family's) computer, and you will not allow it to be used inappropriately in any way. State this as a declaration and then end the discussion, especially if there is a remote chance that it wasn't him. The fire fighting is now complete; you stated the problem and set a boundary.

**An Ongoing Preventive Plan for Success**. Begin by placing the computer used by the kids in a common area that you can regulate and monitor at any time. Computers should not be located in bedrooms. When I bring up this topic at my seminars, parents often complain about not wanting a computer in the dining room or living room. When I was raising my children, I decided to locate the computer in a small sunroom off the kitchen. Certainly, I would have preferred using that room for plants, relaxation, and basking in the sun, but my primary focus was the kids and I'd have more time later in life for setting up the house the way I wanted.

Once the location is set, time frames and rules should be established for computer use. I suggest that each child be given a limited amount of time for non-school use of the computer, monitored and enforced by the parent. If these changes are new for your home, be prepared for objections and opposition. Rather than becoming angry with them, let them vent their frustration. It's also important to set up consequences if time frames are deliberately exceeded or if rules are ignored.

Some parents may have situations in which the kids are home alone and use of the computer cannot be monitored. Although some might disagree, I suggest purchasing filtering or monitoring software that runs on the computer and records the user's actions. During the week, my children usually arrived home before I did. I wanted them to have access to the computer so I purchased and installed one of these monitoring software programs. In one of our weekly family meetings, I revealed to them that I would be installing monitoring software to keep them safe, not because I didn't trust them. I told them that at the end of each day, I would examine the reports that showed me all the Internet activity for the day, including chat conversations, e-mails written and read, and Web sites visited. They weren't happy about it and voiced their objections that it wasn't fair. But it motivated them to discipline themselves on their appropriate use of the computer. Reading the reports each night gave me a feeling of comfort that they were safe. Occasionally I would read a warning to a friend from one of my kids in a chat or e-mail, "Please don't use any swears, my Dad is reading this!"

As of the writing of this expanded edition of the book, technology has made amazing advances that give parents so many more easy-to-use options. From monitoring computer use, to monitoring cell phone activity, parents have the ability to know exactly who their children are communicating with, what they are seeing, and even where their child is with the device. While many adults have disagreed with my position on monitoring, it is my opinion that it is a parent's responsibility to know who his or her child or teen is communicating with and what is being discussed. The child's safety comes before privacy due to the danger of predators.

# A Holiday Survival Guide

The holidays are a time of joy and tradition. Parents are gearing up for family activities, fun and festivals. The kids are getting excited about being home for school vacation. Here are eight tips for ensuring a happier holiday season.

**Good Behavior in Someone Else's Home**. At some point prior to arriving at someone else's home for a holiday party, get to your child's eye level and go over the rules for attending the party. You may even ask the children to explain the rules to you and don't be surprised if they already know. Throughout the event, acknowledge them every time you witness the behavior you want. If their behavior has been a problem in the past, tell them there will be a consequence. If you choose this option, be ready to implement it immediately.

**Reduce the Toys and Gifts**. A few weeks before the holiday season arrives, allow your children to lead an activity to thin out the usable toys and clothes they already have and then donate them to a local charity. Let your child participate in the process, especially the delivery to the donation center. Commit to buying your children fewer toys. Too many can create visual chaos and excessive stimulation, and certainly does not teach crucial lessons of moderation and limits.

**Take Care of Yourself**. When you become stressed over the holidays, frantic and frazzled feelings will impact the children, and they will begin to display over-stimulation in their own way. Take time out to recharge your batteries. You need extra rest, exercise and healthy eating, all of which are necessary in order to exhibit greater self-control and patience.

**Teach Children Gratitude.** (see previous chapter on this topic) Consider getting your family involved in a giving exercise during the holiday season. Donate your time to volunteer for a charitable organization by wrapping presents for a gift collection agency, delivering a meal to a shut-in, or serving the hungry at a soup kitchen. This act of compassion will remain with your children for a very long time. During the Thanksgiving holiday, we as a family would prepare and deliver a meal to an elderly person living alone. I'll never forget the year we delivered our dinner to an elderly lady who was so grateful for our gift, she cried as we left. My son was silent as we drove away and he had tears in his eyes.

**Don't Over-Schedule.** During the holidays we automatically think about wanting to connect and to be with family and friends. But if past holidays do not evoke fond memories because of over-scheduling, reconsider your plans for this year and commit to simplifying the family calendar or take a vacation away from home. This move may require declining some invitations or changing routines. One family we connect with often makes it a point to avoid the holiday rush. They plan plenty of get-togethers throughout the year and then disappear at Thanksgiving and/or Christmas to take cruises, go to Disney, or travel to see family out of state.

**Set Realistic Expectations for the Kids.** Let's face it — November and December are exciting times for the kids and stressful, busy times for you. This guarantees that your children are going to behave differently and it will be a challenge to win their cooperation and remain calm. Clarify your boundaries and rules and be patient when their excitement intervenes. Remind yourself about the true meaning of the holidays; it's not about having the perfect family. A big mistake parents make is remembering the holidays from their childhood and trying to re-create them today.

**Create the Reverence of New Traditions.** Participating in family traditions that were passed down from previous generations can be fun and exciting, but can also add to holiday stress when it requires re-creating complex meals, trips, and events that originally belonged to someone else. Take bold steps to create new traditions for your immediate family that will leave lasting impressions, regardless of how simple they might be. When my children were young, we started a new tradition of allowing the kids to open one gift on Christmas Eve. We intentionally gave them new pajamas in this one special gift, which they would wear to bed that night. Every year thereafter, I came up with amusing and creative ways of disguising the gift to keep them guessing, because they knew what they would find in the packages. Creating new, entertaining traditions and faithfully, consistently celebrating them each year will teach your children how to do it themselves years later for their own families.

**Be the Person You Want Your Children to Be**. Finally, there is no better way to teach your children how to enjoy the holidays than to demonstrate through your own actions and behavior the type of person you want them to be. The most powerful training your children will ever have is the observations they make of your behavior on a daily basis. Work hard to remain calm and loving throughout the holidays. When you find yourself on the threshold of an emotional reaction to someone else's behavior, ask yourself if what you're about to say or do will bring your family closer, or create more distance. Being close, of course, is what the holidays are all about!

# Socializing Your Only Child

Social intelligence is defined as interaction with others and is something that a child develops over time. It comes from experience and learning for the child, and patience and guidance for the parent. Parents want so urgently for their children to play cooperatively with other children but when they see them bullying, fighting, or being pushed around, they panic and fear there is something wrong with their children and are ready to take them to counseling.

A parent sent me an e-mail recently with a call for help. She was beginning to notice that her 5-year-old son was acting inappropriately with a favorite playmate for the past several years. Each play date would start off well, with the two boys acting like the best of friends. But Mom noticed recent changes. It seemed that after an hour or two of play, her son would demonstrate some aggression toward his best buddy by throwing dirt, pushing him down and speaking rudely to him. She wasn't sure what to do, but assumed it was time to stop play dates with the little friend.

My response was to relax a bit and not overreact to this change. I encouraged her to not overemphasize his social skills at this point because he is still learning and developing; thus, his skills are nowhere near an adult level. Sometimes we forget how small they are and expect our children to behave as we do. We also think that their behavior should be at its best all the time. But even adults get too much stimulation and suddenly want a break from an encounter with someone else. For children, the development of social intelligence is similar to finding a power tool that is cool to use. Sometimes they almost have to abuse it to understand its power and how it works. They learn from consequences, especially when they are the host of the date. Just as we do, in order to create balance in their life they learn from the mistakes they make or the abuse of something new.    Here are some suggestions for managing a small child's social behavior:

- Avoid stopping the play dates, simply keep them brief.  Most often they enjoy being with their playmates but as we do, they need breaks, too.

- Pay close attention to the length of time that works best for your child before the inappropriate behavior begins.  Knowing this will help you gauge the best length of time for future play dates.

- The sudden change in your child's demeanor could be his way of saying, "I've had enough of social interaction for today." Check on them regularly and don't become alarmed if best friends are suddenly fighting.  See this as their way of saying "enough."

- If your child begins to act inappropriately, end the play date early and do it without being emotional about it.  Attaching your own issues and energy will add more drama and cloud the whole experience.  Your child needs to see the experience as it is to learn and move on.

- When required to stop a play date because of your child's behavior, tell him what you see by saying something such as, "Looks like you have had enough playtime with Brandon for today."

- Be a detective and look for examples of your child's positive play habits.  Make a big deal of it when you see him acting appropriately; in those situations, it's fine to be happy and excited.

- Between play dates, ask open-ended questions that will allow him to come to his own conclusions about what happened.  Ask him, "What was it like to play with Thomas yesterday?"  "Did you enjoy playing with him?"

- When he is open to learning between play dates, talk about what went well and what didn't.  Ask questions such as, "What was the most fun you had when you were playing with your friend?"  "What wasn't fun about playing with him?"  This will teach him that sometimes things are great and sometimes they are not.

- Demonstrate appropriate social intelligence practices yourself for him to see, especially with the other parent.  A child notices

when the parent isn't getting along with other adults. They easily learn negative social behavior from their caregivers.
- Finally, use the world around you to teach your child effective social skills. Bring her attention to incidents of positive social interaction when you are out in public (the park, the store, others' homes, etc.) or even when watching a movie or television.

Social intelligence forms over time. You're not going to get him to be the perfect host or playmate overnight. Be patient with him and remain calm. Relax. I know that when parents see this kind of behavior, they want to fix it immediately. Some may even feel fearful that their child is going to grow up without social skills, and they feel they have to do something about it now. Remember that there is an invisible connection between you and your child, and she can feel when you are acting uptight about something. This can influence her negatively. It works the same way for adults — when someone close to us is feeling something negative, we can sense it and may even act out ourselves.

# Turning Your Husband into a Dad

A few years back, you turned your boyfriend into a husband. You had a vision in mind about what you wanted in a mate, and hopefully he's fulfilled your expectations. Now you have children together and want that terrific partner to step up to the plate to become the dad you want for your kids. Some men rise to the occasion on their own; some don't. If you're reading this chapter because you would like to see something different at home, you can influence his behavior with some guidance, encouragement and leadership.

Before I share the secrets with you, I want to mention step-fathers separately because they are different and the rules for their behavior are not identical. In the next chapter, I point out that until a natural and loving bond takes place between your husband and your children, you must be the primary adult to administer discipline. Your new husband is there to love, honor and support you. He can participate in creating house rules, enforcing them, and being available to the kids when they need help or guidance.

A primary factor that influences how a man behaves as a father is often the model presented to him as a child in his own home. If his mother took full charge of raising and disciplining the children, then he may imitate that model and sit on the sidelines expecting his wife to do the same. If his father's only active role was as a punitive disciplinarian, then he may do just that. Our childhood has a major influence in shaping our preconceived notions of our role as parents. This is important information for any woman to help her understand her husband's behavior.

I knew a young couple many years ago who had a great marriage. But when the children arrived, they fought and argued too much. She believed that her husband wasn't helping her with the kids; leaving her to do all the parenting while he did other things. She would only take it for so long and then lose her temper, yelling at him. He would turn defensive and then contribute to the argument by yelling back at her, declaring that he works all day and brings home the paycheck. The problem was that they never talked about what they expected from each other. She had a preconceived idea about his behavior as a father. He had a preconceived idea about fatherhood based on the example set by his own father.

Now that I've laid some groundwork for you in understanding your husband's behavior, here are six secrets for turning him into the dad you want your kids to have.

**Examine His Models.** Take the time to understand his parents' behavior when he was growing up. This isn't about faulting them but instead, getting a better understanding of the examples they offered. Talk to his mother if possible and ask how discipline was handled in the family.

**Share Your Expectations.** In a moment that is appropriate for conversation, ask your husband what discipline was like when he was young. Ask him how he sees each of your roles and responsibilities as parents, and then share your expectations with him. In his book *The 7 Habits of Highly Effective People,* author Steven R. Covey advises that we should seek first to understand, and then be understood.

**Create a Parenting Team.** Engage your husband in discussion about parenting as a team. Take opportunities to talk through and agree on discipline methods, rules, and limits when the children aren't around. Hold family meetings and support each other. When a new situation presents itself with the kids, postpone discipline until you've had a chance to discuss it in private. Once you reach agreement, approach the kids as a united front with your decision. If your child comes to you to complain about the other parent, be a good listener. Bring the two together so they can talk it out. If the other parent isn't available, tell your child that you'll discuss it when you're all together again.

**Encourage Him.** When your husband steps up to discipline

appropriately, supports you in front of the kids, or demonstrates even the smallest positive "dad" behavior, encourage him with hugs, kisses, or positive words of encouragement in private. Let him know when you've noticed him doing things well.

**Too Much Correction Creates Discouragement.** If you notice a mistake or not doing something perfectly, let it go. Walk away and avoid the urge to correct or scold him, especially in front of the children. Consistency is more important that perfection.

**Learn to be Better Parents Together.** Finally, be sure that you are not being perceived as an expert or a know-it-all. This could contribute to his feeling of discouragement and shortcomings as a dad. Admit to your husband that your children did not come with an instruction manual and you're both in this together, trying to figure things out on your own. Read this parenting book together or take the Love, Limits, and Lessons parenting class as a couple.

# Tips for an Awesome Step Dad

According to the organization Parenthood in America and at the time of this writing, about half of the 60 million children under 13 in this country are currently living with one biological parent and that parent's current partner. Most studies published in the 1990s predicted that after the year 2000, the number of stepfamilies would outnumber nuclear families, but the 2000 U.S. Census did not include the category. Because many children today live in step-relationships, of which two out of three are predicted to fail, it has become even more important for stepfathers to understand their role, step up to the plate, and do what they can to grow a strong stepfamily. If he can't, it can cause the children to lack the crucial support that enables them to thrive or even survive society's cultural, educational and work challenges. Here are 6 tips for effective step dads.

**Create a Team**. Commit to creating agreements with your spouse. Both adults should reach agreements and understandings in the very beginning about their positions on discipline and on house behaviors and rules. Once common ground has been reached, a family meeting should be held to announce the house rules to the children; these rules should be discussed often and handled consistently.

**Understand Your Role**. Accept that you are not a replacement Dad. The children's natural father will always be their father and you are not taking his place. Have a discussion with your new stepchildren early on to help them understand this. Explain to them that your primary role is to be there to love and honor their mother. You can also share with them that you will be responsible for helping their mother set house rules for behavior, enforcing them and also being available to them when they need help, guidance, or just someone to listen to.

**Guidelines on Discipline**. Except when the children are very young (toddlers), the biological mother should be the primary adult to administer discipline. Until you have developed a strong bond with the children, you should not be in the forefront of parenting. Keeping this in mind will reduce your chances of hearing the phrase, "You're not my father!" However, you can have a say when established house rules have been broken, such as limiting certain behaviors in certain rooms of the house, inappropriate use of furniture or equipment or violations of respect for others. The important thing to keep in mind is establishing these rules up front and keeping them fair and appropriate.

**Create a Bond**. In the nuclear family, there is a natural bond between parents and their biological children. In a stepfamily, that bond must be built up over time. Because, as they say, "blood is thicker than water," it will be especially important for you to begin gradually developing a relationship with your new children. Recognize that the children may exhibit some jealousy as they begin to see that they have to share their mother with someone else. Relax and don't get defensive. See the situation from their perspective and give them plenty of room. Help preserve some "alone time" for them to connect with their mother without you, and don't take their words or actions personally. Make yourself available to them so they can reach out and look for ways that you can connect with them through enjoyable activities, humor, or common interests.

**Be a Role Model**. Begin by committing yourself to always treating their mother with respect. Little boys will grow up learning how to treat girls as they watch their mother being treated. Little girls will grow up learning how to allow themselves to be treated in ways they see their mother treated. Be mindful of how you handle your own frustrations and anger. Little eyes and ears learn through the model you will offer them. If you see situations that frustrate you, walk away and take a break. Initial feelings may overwhelm you and cause you to speak or act in ways that you may regret. Never scold or correct the children's mother in front of them. If you see something that you must bring up with her, find time away from the children to share your feelings. And always remember to talk about the children's natural father respectfully, even if you feel that he doesn't deserve it.

**Actively Build Your New Family**. My final suggestion is to invest in your new family. If this is not your first marriage, learn from prior mistakes and concentrate on doing what's right. In the candle-lighting exercise used in many wedding ceremonies, the lighting of the Unity candle represents two people coming together as individuals, beginning the process of creating a new family. Similarly, your new spouse and her children are an individual unit coming together with you as an individual. Take an active role with your spouse to create new traditions and rituals. Be patient if the children push back and resist your changes. You will have more success at engaging them in the new family unit if you handle resistance with calmness and forgiveness. And don't forget that you can teach a child so much about self-respect by the way you take care of yourself. Taking care of yourself emotionally, spiritually, physically and socially will set examples for your new children. From your own behavior, you will create a model that will stay with them for the rest of their lives.

# The Single Mom's Survival Guide on Discipline

Other than parents of multiples, I'm not sure there is anyone with a tougher parenting job than a single mother, and there are plenty of them. According to the U.S. Census Bureau, there were 13.6 million single parents in 2007 raising 21.2 million children. To provide perspective, that is nearly 26% of children under 21 in the U.S. today. And the Web site About.com reports that 84% of custodial parents are mothers.

Single moms fill my parenting classes looking for help and I've spent many hours with them discussing their frustrations about their role as the sole caregiver. One major mistake they make that leads to discipline problems is using their children to fill their relationship needs. Examples include labeling the oldest male child as "the man of the house" or treating the female children more as girlfriends rather than children. Being a single parent requires the courage to be firm and in control without creating more chaos for the kids. Here are 8 tips on discipline for the single mom.

**Hold Family Meetings.** Children need to feel a part of the team and when they do, they are more likely to cooperate and will misbehave less often. Schedule a consistent day and time each week to sit down with the children to connect with them. The activities that are most effective for these sessions are those that encourage dialogue and sharing. You may also use this time to go over family rules, but don't make this the highlight of the meeting. Once you have demonstrated what the role of the facilitator looks like, allow the kids to take turns being the facilitator themselves, determining the discussion topics and agendas.

**Create Structure, Routines, and Boundaries.** Children need consistency and routine in daily life, especially at a time when the family structure has suddenly changed due to death, separation, or divorce. The more structure they have in their world, the more secure they feel and the less likely they are to misbehave. Some single moms are afraid to create order and limits because they fear the dreaded words from their children, "I want to live with Daddy, he doesn't have so many rules." But it is these rules that will help them become the young adults you want them to be.

**Establish New Traditions.** Take the opportunity to create new traditions and rituals as a family to create special moments and new closeness with the children. Doing so will allow for bonding but will also help obliterate hurtful memories. If the child's other parent is in the picture and visitation is a new norm around the holidays, see the complex scheduling as something positive and not stressful, as well as an opportunity to create new activities or routines.

**Boyfriends Should Not Discipline.** Children sometimes see the new boyfriend as a threat, and experience jealousy. They don't like sharing their mother with other siblings, let alone a stranger. The boyfriend is there for mom and not for the children, so I encourage single moms who are dating to set up rules from the start that the boyfriends should not have any disciplinary role. It is perfectly fine for him to find special ways to connect with the kids with fun, play, and games, but the discipline should be left to mom.

**Engage Male Family Members for Boys.** It is a fact that boys who have male role models in their lives mature in emotionally healthy ways. Boys need men as mentors. If there is no active and present father in a boy's life, I suggest that single moms find ways of setting up extra time with male relatives to reach out to her boys. This would let the relatives know how valuable they are and encourage them to spend time with her boys to help them grow into young men.

**Speak Respectfully About Their Father.** Regardless of a

mother's feeling toward her ex-husband, to the children he is still their father and still someone they may look up to. The children may not truly understand what the breakup was all about, and certainly don't see the world the way their mother does. It is important that mom should always speak respectfully about him to the children. If she doesn't, they may become angry at her and become more sympathetic toward their father as an act of defense. This kind of inappropriate behavior on mom's part also models backbiting and sabotage for the children. Mom should keep her negative emotions about the children's father to herself and not confide in the kids. Close friends and therapists are best for this.

**Take Care of Yourself**. When a flight attendant on an aircraft demonstrates the oxygen mask, she always instructs passengers to put on their mask first and then help their children. This illustration demonstrates how a single mother must first take measures to care for herself so that she can effectively take care of the children. With an already over-extended schedule, it may seem impossible for a single mom to take time out to take care of herself. But if she truly wants to be the best mom for her kids, she must find a way to make it happen.

# When Your Ex (or Your Mother) Parents Differently

The first thing you should do if your children go to another parent's home part-time is to ask that other parent for his or her cooperation in establishing similar rules to yours. The fact is that if a child consistently sees familiar rules and boundaries in multiple environments, they are more likely to become more cooperative, quickly. In some family situations, that "other parent" may be a grandparent or an after-school caregiver and the same applies; ask them to join you in using similar discipline, rules, and parenting practices. But there is a risk that the other caregiver may not choose to support you in this manner, especially if your relationship with him or her is not healthy. If this is the case and their "parenting" is not posing a danger to your child, there may not be anything you can do about their poor choices while your child is in their care.

**Establish Firm Rules and Boundaries**. We cannot control what someone else does in their environment but we do have the power to control our own. That means taking the time and making the effort to set up firm and clear boundaries with our children and doing it without anger or emotion. This is where frequent family meetings come in to play. I suggest that parents take time to think of all the important boundaries they want to have for their children and then establish a set of rules that should be addressed in a meeting. If any of the parent's rules include devices that must remain in the home, such as handheld video games and cell phones, the parent may have to verify that those items are not leaving the house with the child. Likewise, the parent may have to verify that unacceptable items, such as video games and cell phones, are not coming into the house when the child returns. I frequently hear from parents who do not allow their child to have a cell phone, that the other parent provides one for the child against the other parent's wishes. Remember that you have the right to keep your child safe from things that may endanger him and have the right to take that item away.

**Your Behavior Will Help Your Child Adapt**. One of the characteristics of society that creates a challenge for parents today is that discipline and parenting are done differently in different households or environments. When we were children, adults seemed to treat us the same. This motivated us to comply and cooperate with little resistance. Parenting is different today and children use the differences in the treatment they get from their caregivers to their advantage. This means that your child will most likely challenge you when he returns to your home of rules and boundaries, after spending a weekend at the other parent's house with unlimited television, video games or his favorite junk foods. Your behavior during the transition period of your child returning to your home is crucial to the child adapting successfully back into your home structure. Know that he or she will attempt to get you to change your boundaries to match the ones in the other home.

**Do Not Get Angry**. I know, easier said than done, right? Especially so when your child is getting angry and throwing the insults because you run a tighter ship than the other parent. But I encourage you to not lose sight of the fact that it isn't the child's fault. If you examine why you may be getting angry, it might help you calm down. One reason is because your parents would never have allowed you to speak up and act out the way you're allowing your child to speak up. Another reason is that it hurts so much when you hear your child defend the other parent when that adult may have behaved badly toward you in the previous relationship. A third may be that you are feeling resentful for all the things you've done for your child and here he or she is, throwing insults at you. One more might be that fear is rising up inside of you, making you fearful of one day hearing the words from your child, "I want to go live with Dad (or Mom) because it's more fun at their house; or worse, "They love me more!"

**Remain Steadfast in Your Parenting.** You may find yourself quick to loosen up your discipline at home, hoping to ease the stress associated when your child returns from the other parents home. Don't do it! If your child makes statements that the other parent lets her do the things you won't, just agree with her by saying, "I know he (she) does." Reinforce your agreement with something like, "But in this house we do it differently," and then just walk away. Your child may attempt to argue with you to get you to change your boundaries. And one very important point; avoid criticizing what the other parent or caregiver is doing in their home. Say nothing about what appears to be going on because doing so will only provide more ammunition for your child to dislike you and want to fight more.

**Your Child Will Adapt.** It is a fact that you may have to re-establish rules with a child whenever he comes back to you from a different home where things aren't being done as you would want them done. If the child throws a fit because he isn't adapting to your house rules every time he comes back to you, relax and let him have the meltdown. Believe it or not, children crave "sameness" and routine. When routine is changed frequently from household to household, they don't like it and it can trigger anger and tantrums. Be patient with your child and take comfort in knowing that what you are doing is right. Your peacefulness, calmness, and consistency will help him adapt gradually.

# Getting Kids to Clean Their Room

My wife and I don't have the time to watch much TV, but one program running on NBC that caught our eye recently is the television show PARENTHOOD. I'm bringing this up because there are many scenes that represent classic parenting situations; some handled well and some not so well. I remember one scene involving the youngest son Crosby, played by Dax Shepard and his 6-year-old son Jabbar, well played by Tyree Brown. Jabbar began to act overwhelmed and helpless when his father asked him to clean up his room. Crosby then moved the request up a few notches, to demands and threats, but to no avail. A little while later, the boy's mother arrived home and discovered that Crosby ended up cleaning Jabbar's room for him and a fight between the parents erupted; a realistic incident that can happen in many families.

**Defining the Problem.** I believe there are three primary causes of the messy room; children and teens lack organizational skills, they are enjoying exerting power over their own space, or they are purposely keeping their room a mess as a way of getting even with an over controlling or unengaged parent or caretaker. I have outlined some tips for parents on what to do about each of these issues, but we must first examine why this becomes a battle ground between parents and children.

Many parents are in a struggle over the messy room because they know how important it is to allow a child or teen to have their personal space, yet they feel the space is being abused by keeping it untidy. Other adults come from a position of fear that their child or teen will grow up to be a slob if they don't get them to become more organized with their room or possessions now. And then there are other parents and caregivers who see the child's messy room as just another form of not complying with the adults. Some adults are drawn back to the feelings they had as a child when they were forced to clean their room or punished for not keeping it clean. When they see their child's unkempt room, it conjures up these bad feelings and then think to themselves, "My parents wouldn't have allowed me to get away with a having a messy room."

**Forcing a Child Doesn't Work Today.** While force may have been a normal parenting approach in autocratic times, it doesn't work today. Forcing a child to keep his or her room clean might get you what you want, but it will also destroy your relationship with your child or teen. It might seem like it's working, but there is a good chance your child will find a way to sabotage the relationship in other ways as a means for revenge against the force you use in your parenting. Below are four tips that don't include the use of force.

**Teach Them While They're Young.** Give young children small tasks to do to help keep their room picked up. Telling a child to go clean her room is like saying to her, "Go explore space." Like in the television show example above, it can easily overwhelm and frustrate them. The success they experience with small and repetitive tasks can motivate them to want to do more and also creates a foundation of good feelings around keeping their room clean. These will still be with them when they become teens and can influence how well they keep their room picked up then. Toys can create chaos so things work best if they are kept in a playroom separate from the child's bedroom. This may not be possible for everyone, so at least consider separating toys into two categories; chaos and supervised. Chaos toys are the large, easy-to-pick up items that are usually kept in a toy box. A daily routine can be established for picking up these toys before dinner or bed. Supervised toys are the sets or kits that include lots of small pieces, such as building and play sets. These should be kept out of a child's reach so they can ask for permission to play with them with the parent's approval. It is also very helpful to establish rules for playing with these types of toys, such as where they will be played with and when they will be picked up and put back in the container.

**Set Up Rules About What Can Go Into a Bedroom.** When it comes to messy rooms, some parents are appropriately concerned about the safety and wellbeing of their child, such as used dinner ware, dirty laundry, or uneaten food amidst the papers, books, clothing, and toys on the floor of the child's room. If a parent establishes rules about what is and is not acceptable for the child to bring into his room, then this eliminates a huge portion of the concern. Announce a set of rules that food, dishes and such are no longer allowed in the bedroom. You can also declare that friends will be allowed in the room (or even just over to play) when the room is picked up. Turn over the responsibility of doing laundry to older children by providing instructions on using the laundry machines. Set up rules that expensive electronic devices with access to the Internet are no longer allowed in the child's bedroom without supervision, such as iPods, tablets, Kindles, and laptop computers.

If you have used some of these suggestions and more, and still your child's room is a mess, remember that your child's room belongs to your child. Pick your battles because some are more important than others. You also want to ask yourself, "Is it more important for me to have clean rooms in my house or a strong relationship with my child?" When we get to where we're going at the end of this life and we find ourselves facing the greater power that created the magic of life, do you think he'll really say to us, "Nice job, you made sure that your child's room was clean all the time."

# Your Child's Report Card Comes Home

If you made the decision as a parent to behave differently than your parents did then kudos to you. Too many adults repeat the mistakes of their own parents by treating their children in a similar manner. Many of us (but not all) had parents who were harsh and abrasive toward us when we brought our less-than-perfect report card home to show them and obtain their signature. Not all families were like this and if you were treated fairly and respectfully by your folks, then good for you. But it was common in families from generations past to just repeat what their parents did to them. They used punishment and fear to motivate their children to do better in school. I remember my mother's cautionary warning of, "Wait until your father gets home," after reviewing my imperfect grades. The punishment administered by my father was a standard number of licks from a belt for each grade lower than a B; the lower the grade, the higher number of whippings. I waited in fear up in my room, sometimes for hours, moving from thoughts of "how to change the grade on my report card," to thoughts of running away from home before the next marking period. I can assure you that experiencing the fear of the impending punishment never generated thoughts of "how I can bring my grades up," although that's exactly what my parents were probably hoping for.

**Letting Fear Determine the Outcome**. I'm probably safe in guessing that most parents no longer use spanking as a discipline tool today to help their kids get better grades in school, but what they do use instead may still not be getting the results they're hoping for. Adults like my parents used fear to drive the discipline they used with my seven siblings and me. They were afraid that we were not taking school seriously and may do poorly, so they used this fear to pass more fear onto us. Parents today may not spank, but they let their fear of their kids' failure determine the discipline such as yelling, punishing, grounding, and taking away privileges. My word of caution is, don't do this. Modern-day scholars tell us that the negative things we allow ourselves to feel and think about, will expand. In other words, if you continue to believe you're a victim in life, more incident will happen to you to reinforce that belief. If you complain about what's not right in your life, you'll get more of the same. And if you continue to allow yourself to fear that your children will fail in school, they will live up to your expectation. And then if you force your children to continue to feel the fear you're passing on to them, that too will expand. They will grow up to become more fearful and it will be that emotion that will determine how they live.

**Prelude to the Report Card.** Now that I've told you what NOT to do, here is my suggestion on what TO DO instead. This formula I'm laying out works best with school-age children through adolescence. First begin by setting your children up for success with the one piece of their school work that you have greater influence over; the homework. Begin by taking your child shopping for school supplies. This means letting them hold the money and carry the hand basket. Stay with them and guide (not control) them on what to buy. Allowing them to pay at the cash register completes the feeling of ownership of the supplies and eventually the process of doing the homework. Next, help them set up the space where they will do their homework. Depending on your child's learning style and temperament, both a main traffic area in the dining room and being hidden away in their room may not work. Find a happy medium that both of you can agree on and build that space with adequate desk space and lighting. The final piece is helping your child establish a schedule on doing the homework; what time it will begin and for how long. Some children need a break between coming home from school and beginning their work. Determine what will work best with your child, document it, and then stick to it.

**Establish the "Quiet Time" and Keep it No Matter What.**

The window carved out for homework should also be marked as a declared "quiet time" of no entertainment electronics. This means banning Facebook, Internet, Nintendo, movies, cell phones, home telephone, or television during this time. Setting up this boundary will help your child concentrate. A young person who knows the rule of no entertainment electronics during the homework window will be less likely to be tempted to turn to it when the task at hand becomes difficult or boring. Because many schools now put textbooks online, I advise parents to have a "family computer" located in a common area for the child or teen to use to access their books. And because of the easy access to inappropriate material on the Internet, the location of the computer should be one in which the parents can monitor the child's or teen's usage.

The most difficult aspect of creating and keeping this "quiet time" is one that many parents may have difficulty with or even disagree with; keeping it in place even on days when there is no homework assigned. It is common for some children or teens to be faced with the decision of, "Do I do my homework even though it is due by the end of the week, or do I play with the newest video game that I'm addicted to?" When faced with this dilemma, many will "snow plow" their homework assignments and then panic the night before they are due. Keeping the "quiet time" in place Monday through Thursday, in spite of no homework assignments due the next day, helps to avoid this problem. If the child or young teen has no homework on a particular day, the only quiet time activities allowed should be reading, writing, or anything creative and quiet that do not include the banned items I listed previously.

**Sharing the Report Card.** When your child brings the report card home, begin by doing three important things during the encounter; allow your child to hold the card and read the grades to you, remain completely quiet during the reading, and listen with 100% of your attention. Once the reading is complete, do not pass judgment or invoke consequences or punishment. Your job as a parent is to ask open ended questions that will allow your child to make his own assessment (not yours) of his performance being reflected in the report card. Ask your child questions such as; What is your favorite grade from this marking period, Why, What is your least favorite grade, and Why. Acknowledge any joy you see in her face about a particular subject she did well in, by telling her what you see. For example, if she exhibits excitement about her grade in math, simply say to her, "You look pretty proud of your math skills, what do you think helped you get such a good grade." If he appears to be sad while talking about a low grade in science, ask him, "What would you have liked that grade to be instead?" When he provides you with an answer, ask him what he could do to bring that grade up for the next marking period.

Please take note, your child's homework and report card belongs to him or her, not you. A parent who uses too much control over a child and what that child owns, will end up raising a child who is less likely to take ownership of things he should, and avoid self-responsibility.

# Teaching Children about Money

Our children today have little concept of money. They see us pull out "the card" for most purchases or press a few buttons at the automated teller machine to access what they think is an endless supply of cash. And when our children see us purchasing luxuries such as a 42" plasma screen, the latest fancy cell phone, or a GPS for the car, they don't understand why we won't buy them the latest toy.

For a moment, imagine this scene: an adult and child are in a store and the adult tells the child "no" to a purchase he wants. The child then throws himself on the floor in a fit because mom won't buy him the toy. Mom then gets upset and feels resentful that her child doesn't appreciate all she's done for him. In the back of her mind she thinks about all she's purchased in spite of the fact that she struggles to get by with the little money she brings in each month. Her feelings of resentment then turn into anger and she yells at him that he doesn't appreciate the toys he just received for his birthday a few weeks ago. His fit then turns into a tantrum and, before you know it, she's scolding him or even spanking him to stop his tantrum. She can't handle the scene any longer and either drags him off to the parking lot or gives in and buys him the toy. Within a few days or weeks, she calls my office to find out when my next parenting class is. She's tired of these episodes and doesn't know what else to do.

Children can't possibly know what our financial burdens and obligations are. We should not expect them to and we certainly shouldn't be using guilt to make them feel bad for not appreciating what we buy them. Instead, we should avoid buying our children (and ourselves) too much in order to model living within our means. We should also institute and maintain a plan in the family to teach our children how to handle money appropriately. Here are steps to one possible solution.

**Setting up a Tool.** Place four yellow mailing envelopes that measure approximately 6" x 9" in a 2 or 3-ring binder. The exact size of the envelopes doesn't really matter, as long as they are big and strong enough to contain dollars and coins. Allow your child to personalize the binder with special drawings about money. Avoid telling your child how to decorate the binder and allow him to create what naturally comes to mind about money. Each envelope will have a percentage and a title.

**The Envelopes.** The first envelope should be titled TITHING or DONATIONS and should have 10% on it. Making this envelope first will teach your child that giving money away to others in need comes before satisfying personal desires. If you are not a religious person, tithing doesn't have to mean giving to a church. The money in this envelope can be used to give to any charity.

The second envelope should be titled SPENDING and have 20% on it. Money in this envelope can be used anytime your child wants to spend money. For example, children can use this money when going on shopping trips with an adult or when the ice cream truck is in the neighborhood.

The third envelope should be titled SHORT TERM SAVINGS and have 30% on it. Money saved in this envelope is saved for something the child may wish for and can purchase within a year or two, such as a new toy, game cartridge, or spending money for a school trip. Allow your child to draw or cut out a picture to represent what he is saving for and paste it onto the envelope. You may even want to put the price of this item on the envelope as a target savings amount.

The fourth and last envelope should be titled LONG TERM SAVINGS and have 40% written on it. Money saved in this envelope should be removed and banked on a monthly or quarterly basis. I suggest there be no target for this except to save and record the deposits as they are made. You may even want to make a rule that this money can only be withdrawn with your permission.

**Implementing the Practice.** Every time your child receives money as a gift or a monetary reward for service, it should be broken down by the percentages on the envelopes and deposited into them. Parents may want to build a cash box and store it away, ready for making change for the envelopes. Implementing this practice with your child, even if she is too young for math, will begin to teach her about percentages and will help establish a foundation for savings and spending. When the family goes to church, allow the child to empty whatever is in the TITHING envelope and bring it along to donate. If you don't attend a church, then on occasion, allow your child to donate the contents to a charity.

**Chores and Allowance.** I do not support children getting allowances. I believe that parents will be more successful at raising cooperative kids if everything the children does to help out is NOT rewarded with money. I recommend that parents identify basic chores that every child should do without reward. These should be done for the simple fact of cooperating and contributing to the home and the family. Children can however, be rewarded financially when completing assignments that go above and beyond basic helping chores, such as working in the yard, helping to clean or organize the basement, or helping a parent with an office or paper-based task like filing papers.

World renowned inspirational speaker and bestselling author, Dr. Wayne Dyer, has a wonderful book for parents to read to their children about money. The book, *It's Not What You've Got! Lessons for Kids on Money and Abundance* (Hay House Publishing, 2007), expands on ten valuable lessons we can teach our children about money.

# "Knock it off or I'll give you something to cry about!"

We are emotional creatures and so are our children. When our children have an emotional outburst over something, it can drive us crazy. I am often asked, "How long should I allow my child to express her emotions before I send her to her room to whine." My answer is, avoid stopping the expression. Even parents who do the right thing and support a child in expressing her emotions, sometimes think that there should be a limit to how long the expression should continue.

Children have extended outbursts of emotional expression for a reason and parents should avoid getting annoyed and angry with the child. The parent oftentimes even has the power to create the outbursts. I suggest that parents not limit the outburst unless it is in public and is interfering with others. Only then, in a loving and peaceful manner, the child should be removed to a place where he can continue the meltdown without disturbing others. The parent should not talk except to acknowledge what the child might be feeling by saying something like "you look frustrated," or "you look like you're mad at mom." If the tantrum is happening at home the parent should leave the room as long as there are no safety issues in leaving the child alone. If the parent feels that the emotional outbursts are lasting longer than they should, she should consult the child's pediatrician or a therapist for help.

Teaching a child to simply not dwell on things can also be beneficial and it is HOW you do it that is the key. Getting a child (or even an adult) to stop focusing on an emotion cannot be accomplished successfully through force or control; there are far more effective and healthier ways of accomplishing this goal. Control might get a child to stop dwelling on it for the moment, but the result is that whatever it is she is feeling (and it might be a totally different emotion than what the caregiver actually sees) will get stuffed and attempt to resurface at a later time. Or the child will feel resentment toward the caregiver for forcing the stuffed emotion, thereby creating a NEW emotion that didn't exist before. The most important question the caregiver should ask them self before attempting to stop the dwelling, is "why is this emotion occurring." Sometimes young children appear to be dwelling on something familiar to them, such as a boo-boo, when in fact, the emotion is completely different.

While waiting to begin a training session with preschool teachers late one afternoon, I watched a mother enter the school for pick-up and interact with her preschooler as they prepared to go home. The little girl rushed to her mother in tears and exclaimed, "Mommy, I have a boo-boo." Having been through my parenting class (and feeling the pressure to do it right with me standing nearby), the mother got down to her little girl's eye-level, acknowledged her feelings and said, "It looks like your finger might hurt." The little girl put her hand down and then seemed to be searching the room. She focused on a set of toys in the corner of the room and then said, "No... they wouldn't let me play with those toys today!" The mother then looked over at the toys and said, "You look disappointed that you couldn't play with your favorite toys." The little girl was silent for just a moment and then began to cry as she said, "No... I wanted daddy to pick me up today." Mom then said, "You look like you miss daddy." The little girl nodded and fell into her mother's embrace. I later learned that daddy had made a promise to his daughter that he would pick up the little girl, but a long meeting forced him to call his wife to pick up the child. The little girl's feeling of disappointment started with a boo-boo and then jumped to the toys, both with histories of familiar emotion for her. It may have been difficult for her to get her arms around the missing daddy feeling.

Identifying and handling emotions can be difficult for children. They feel this thing inside of them and it can be frightening. That's why I always coach parents to help their child identify the problem by simply sharing what the parents sees from their perspective. They should not assume they know what it is, just tell the child what they see. This acknowledgment should also include mirroring back the facial expression. The parent can say things like, "you look like you miss your brother," or "you look like you're mad at mommy." Parents (or teachers) can also get a child to stop dwelling on the emotion by not dwelling on it themselves. The child looks to the parent's balanced reaction as a way of helping learn self-regulation of emotional states.

Parents can teach their children how to self-regulate so that when emotion rises up in the future, they will be more prepared to deal with it. When children sense the emotional arousal, they will be motivated to reach for their blanket to comfort them. If they sense the arousal of fear over a frightening image or interaction, they will be able to manage themselves by averting their eyes or moving to another location. In the end, experts state that children who are taught to be aware of distressing arousal and to self-regulate their emotions, are more likely to have healthier social relationships, act out appropriately, and demonstrate less aggression.

## Are You Raising a Connected Child or a Clingy Child?

If I had to pick one chapter of this book as a key chapter to the concepts I teach, this one would be it. It represents the primary foundation of all of my parenting principles in raising the kind of child who will very likely go on to find his or her purpose in life, on schedule, and change the world. It deals with a problem that many parents experience that may be a symptom of a deeper rooted problem from the child's first few years of life.

Clinginess of toddlers and preschoolers is a somewhat common problem that can be added to the list of challenging behaviors. Sometimes, it's even school-age children who are clingy and they just won't leave the mother alone. It can make her feel suffocated and annoyed and before you know it, she's snapping at her child and feeling bad about the relationship. It then gets worse because the child can feel her frustration and the child gets equally frustrated, wanting to connect with the mother even more.

**What's Going on in the Brain.** According to experts such as pediatrician Dr. William Sears, the first 12 months of a baby's life is the most critical time for the development of the brain. It lays a foundation for how that child will view his or her world as he or she develops and grows. That foundation will also determine what kind of relationships the child will develop as the child matures. Although many authors and psychologists will tell you they do, infants do not require discipline in the first 12 – 18 months, they simply need to be cared for and have their needs met. During this first 12 month period, brain cells, known as neurons, are forming what becomes the "wiring" for the baby to organize and store information. The more the baby's needs are met swiftly, the more complete his wiring becomes.

**Herein Lies the Problem.** Psychologists tell us about something that occurs in the first year of life called object permanence; if an object a baby is looking at is suddenly hidden from sight, the baby thinks it is permanently gone. Have you ever played peek-a-boo with a baby? When you first hide your face, he appears to be concerned and startled, but when you reveal your face again, he smiles or giggles. The same thing happens with people. If a baby's mother disappears for hours at a time, the baby believes that she's permanently gone and the baby may begin to feel anxious and fear that their caregiver and nurturer is really gone. This affects the development of the "wiring" of the baby's brain and can lead to a greater sense of disconnection as she develops. The result may be her inability to trust, turning her into a clingy child during the toddler and preschool years, and even affecting the quality of trust, empathy, intimacy and a sense of self later in her adult life.

**Raising a Connected Child.** One big step in helping your child to become more connected is to avoid putting her in overwhelming situations where both of you will fail. One example is the grocery or department store, an example of fitting the child into our life rather than adjusting our life for our child. She doesn't understand having to pay for things that are sitting right there on the shelf and the shopping experience gets worse if she is hungry or over tired. You end up yelling at her because of her uncooperative behavior. This destroys the parent-child relationship, contributing to disconnection in the child.

**Tips for raising a connected child:**
- Allow healthy physical and emotional attachment to occur during the first 12 months
- Touching, holding, and regular physical contact is critical to the connected child's growth
- Take the time to set up boundaries and limits in advance
- Establish structure at home with gates and baby-proofing devices
- Change your home/life to fit the toddler, not force the toddler to fit your home/life

• Let them be frustrated and work out their own challenges (help at times but don't rescue)

**Children Who Are Connected.** In his book *The Successful Child* (2002, Little Brown & Co), Dr. William Sears asks us to imagine a group of teens at a party who begin to pair off and start "making out." One particular "connected" teen whose parents have taught her to respect her feelings by responding to them appropriately over the span of her childhood, suddenly feels pressured into a sexual situation that she's not ready for and feels confused and scared. Forced to choose between the peer pressure of the moment and trusting her own feelings, she stops the encounter and calls her parents for a ride home. Don't you hope that your teen will make the same choice on her own? If you answered yes, than ask yourself if you're doing today what is required to raise a connected child. Here are few other examples of how a connected child behaves. She…

• Is less likely to experience a fear of strangers
• behaves more cooperatively for the parent
• accepts being left off at preschool without a meltdown
• explores more freely and with bravery
• is likely to be open to new objects and experiences
• is more likely to internalize the wisdom, guidance, and modeling of the parents
• has a stronger development of her emotional intelligence
• is able to interpret the emotions of others and can detect the "red flags"
• possesses a stronger sense of what is right and what is wrong
• has the capacity to trust and care about trustworthy adults

**Are You a Connected Parent?.** If you had any uneasy feelings while reading the paragraphs above or are still frustrated over what it takes to raise a connected child, then perhaps you need some reconnection for yourself. To raise a connected child requires creating some internal balance and peacefulness. Accept the fact that life is not winning the "rat race" that we find ourselves in. Life is about finding more peace and calmness inside of us to better enjoy the limited time we have with our children. Consider slowing down our pace a bit and finding time to take better care of yourself through classes and workshops. Your children don't care how much money you make, they want instead to simply know that you are there and how much you care for them. Caring for others starts with caring for yourself.

# How Adults Teach Children to Lie

A mom recently told me she had been using praise to motivate her three-year-old daughter to stay dry through the night. If the little girl awoke each morning with a dry diaper, her mom would praise her. One particular morning the child apparently took off her diaper and brought it to her mom to show the great results and receive her praise. But later that morning, mom found the REAL diaper that was worn that night–hidden in the child's bedroom and wet! I don't normally support praise, although the exception can be when working with toddlers and preschoolers. Praise can be effective when teaching something new that may be difficult for very young children to master. Praise can give them confidence and motivate them to cooperate with you. The acceptable form of praise in these cases is in expressing delight for your child's accomplishment but avoiding labeling them as a good boy or girl. Adults must be cautious because the side effects of this praise can be motivation to do whatever it takes to get more. From the child's perspective, having a caregiver express delight in something you have accomplished feels great and you usually want to get more.

**We teach them to lie to get our approval.** In the case I above, the little girl loved the praise she was getting for her dry diaper in the morning and learned to hide the wet diaper to please her mother. Even though this example was about a young child, children of all ages learn quickly about getting our approval at all costs. The caregiver's approval feels good and a child will do whatever he can to get it.

My parents obtained their parenting tools from their parents. The penalty my siblings and I received for the C's, D's, and F's on school papers was a whipping from a belt. Because my parents used fear to motivate us to perform, fear is what I felt as a child. To protect myself from what I feared most, I quickly learned how to change grades on papers, hide or destroy my work, or lie about the grades I received on assignments. I often think about where I might be today academically if my parents had responded differently.

Hopefully you are not using old tools our parents may have used on us. But think about how you respond to your children when their performance is not where you think it should be. How do you react emotionally and physically when they make mistakes, make poor decisions, or explore the world? If you yell, get angry, punish, or demonstrate other forms of disapproval, might you be teaching them to lie?

**Parents force their children to be nice to others.** Have you ever told your child to be nice to a playmate or relative, or forced them to say they're sorry? Young children don't always see other children as equals. The process of developing social skills takes time and patience. When one child is mean or disrespectful toward a sibling or playmate, it usually is an indication that they have had enough of the other child and it is time for a break or an end to the playtime. But parents usually admonish their child for the behavior and force their child to be nice. At that particular moment, the child may not have any warm feelings for the other child nor feel sorry in any way.

When I was a child I had an elderly relative I did not like. She smelled terrible and when we went to visit her my parents forced me to give her a hug. It was an excruciating experience and I hated having to go near her. Does this scenario sound familiar? Many of us probably had a similar experience because our parents expected us to show our respect. But at what cost?

**Children learn from the example adults set.** Your child runs to answer the ringing telephone as you shout out, "If it's grandma, tell her that I'm not home." You tell the ticket taker at the admission gate of the amusement park that your child is an age just under the price break so that you can save a few dollars. I know that I have been guilty myself of a few incidents where I taught my son or daughter to lie.

One day my young daughter and I were returning home from a brief shopping trip to get some groceries we needed for dinner. When my daughter saw the ice cream vendor outside the supermarket, her pleading for a small treat pulled at my heartstrings. I caved to her request. I then taught my daughter to lie when I told her not to tell her mother when we got home. I knew that I would be scolded by my wife if she found out I had given our daughter a treat before dinner. It didn't matter anyway. My cover was blown when my daughter walked into the house and said, "We had an ice cream at the store, Mommy." By natural design children have a drive for honesty, but through modeling, training, and getting their needs met, they can easily learn to lie.

In my parenting classes I sometimes poll my participants about the top ten characteristics they want their children to have as an adult. The majority of the time, honesty ranks among the top three. Yet look at the things adults do that promote their children to lie. The mother who found the hidden wet diaper asked me what she should do about her three-year-old hiding it and lying to her. I told her that she should have revealed to her daughter that mommy had found that diaper and now knew that her little girl did not wake up dry.

In the book *Nurture Shock* (Twelve, 2009), authors Po Bryson and Ashley Merryman advise that lying is not just an innocent childhood trait. They believe that parents must let their children know that it is not okay to lie. If we don't, the lying will progress throughout the child's development years. How the parent lets the child know that lying is not okay is the most important factor. If done without a trace of punishment or anger, and instead with a demonstration of acceptance and unconditional love, the child will have less motivation to continue the lying. Her internal compass of integrity will develop naturally as it should.

# Eight Tips for Raising Tweens and Teens

Someone once said that raising a teenager is like trying to nail Jell-O to a tree, and I agree. After raising three of my own and teaching discipline classes since 1995, I'm convinced that nothing prepares a parent for the days when their child becomes an adolescent. All the things you learned when they were a challenge as a preschooler have to be re-learned and used in slightly different ways. Here are 8 tips for success with teens and tweens.

**Hang Out With Them Often.** Communicating and connecting with teens is difficult. They don't communicate directly, they don't talk much, and they are convinced they know more than you do. Look for times just to be with them without too many expectations. I used to knock on my daughter's door and ask if "now was a good time to hang out." She would be painting her nails, writing in her journal, or listening to music and would look at me rolling her eyes and saying, "I guess." Many times I would just sit or lie on her bed and listen to the music with her. Once I let her paint my toenails and we had such a great laugh about it. The only problem was that the guys at the gym had a great laugh too when they saw my feet in the locker room the next day!

**Let Them Have the Last Word.** When you've set a boundary or a limit and they attempt to engage you in argument or ask you why the limit has been set, state it clearly and without anger and let it go. When they attempt to get the last word in, let them. They are doing it purposely to get you to crack and give in.

**Examine the Model You Are Setting.** If you see a behavior you don't like, be sure it's not one they've learned from you or someone in the home. I've spoken to incarcerated men in the prisons and I've told them that their sons will learn how to treat little girls by the way they see their father treat their mother. You are a living, breathing model for your children to learn from.

**Know Your Teen's Friend's Parents**. It's important that we know what influences our teens will have in other families' homes. I always made a point to meet the parents of my children's friends, especially before I allowed them to go to those other homes. When my kids asked permission to go to parties, I would drive them over to the "party house" the day of the get-together or earlier to meet the parents and get a feeling for the environment so that I would know if my kids were going to be safe. My kids detested me doing that and rolled their eyes or huffed as we entered the driveway. But I knew it was my job as a parent to scope out where they would be hanging out. I also reserved the right to not allow them to visit other homes if I disapproved of the people and entertainment.

**Monitor Their Activities**. It's a parent's right and responsibility to know about their teens' involvement in interests and activities. In the chapter on inappropriate use of the Internet, I wrote about how I had installed a monitoring program that recorded all e-mails, Web sites, and chat conversations, and in the evening hours before bedtime, I would sit down and read the log files to "be in the know" about what my kids did. Occasionally, one of their friends would use a cuss word or introduce a topic my kids knew I wouldn't approve of. I would then read my teen's comment: "Hey, don't talk like that, my dad is reading this!"

**Teach Them Respect by Showing It First**. Adults today are so eager to say that kids today have no respect. They often base this on a comparison with how our parents taught us, through force and control. I believe that genuine respect is taught first by modeling it for our children, not forcing them to perform it. You can begin teaching your children respect at any age by knocking on their bedroom door before entering, asking for their time to talk without demanding it, and refraining from disciplining them in front of their friends.

**Let Them Believe They Know More Than You.** You're not going to win this one; they are wired by nature to go through this stage. Let it be our little secret that they really don't know more than we do. Humor them and don't take it so personally when they behave as they do. In order to encourage my son to listen to me, I learned to preface whatever I had to say with, "Can I say a silly dad thing?" Saying that one simple thing before I would give him some advice seemed to give him permission to hear me and follow through.

**Set Clear Boundaries and Keep Them.** Finally, it's critical that we put well-designed boundaries in place for our teens and to keep them. Avoid arbitrary limits that don't make any sense or are created "just because I said so." If you need some time to think, ask for it. If you're not sure about the fairness of a limit, talk it over with the other parent or with a professional. When you set a boundary and then allow the boundary to be removed, sometimes just to get them to leave you alone, you are teaching them that you and your boundaries are not authentic. It's crucial to put your limit in place and keep it. Your teen will also learn how to set and keep solid boundaries for themselves!

With all that being said, you should feel empowered to modify limits and boundaries as your child matures. Make this announcement up front so your children will know that limits at the current age may change as they get older and gain more life experiences. Replace your "NOs" to requests for more freedoms and privileges with the phrase, "I'm not ready for you to do that." If they ask you when you will be ready, simply tell them you're not sure. When one of my daughters was a tween, she asked me to ease up on rule I had in place. When I told her that I wasn't ready to modify it, she asked me how she would know when I was ready. I told her that she should just check in with me occasionally and ask.

# My Teenage Son Won't Come out of His Room

And so goes the question I received from a mother recently. She added that he had become lazy since school got out, spends too much time playing video games, and refuses to play any sports or other athletic activities. Her biggest concern was her worry about what he was doing in his room and asked me if she should force him to keep his door open.

**The Modern Day Teenager.** The fact is that teenage boys tend to become more absent and hide from their parents in their room. This behavior in many boys is normal. In his book *Get Out of My Life, but first could you drive me and Cheryl to the mall?* (Farrar, Straus and Giroux, 2002), Anthony E. Wolf, Ph.D. describes modern day teenagers in how they develop an allergy to their parents; boys are more likely to withdraw more to their room to separate themselves from their parents and girls tend to battle. This separation during adolescence is necessary for the teen to eventually move to the next level of maturity.

**What About Girls?** For the number of mothers coming to me for help with sons locked in their bedrooms, I have an equal number of women coming to me for help with their argumentative and sometimes insulting daughters. Like boys, girls retreat to their rooms to some extent, but they are more likely than boys to verbally and physically challenge their parents. Dr. Anthony reveals in his book that teenage girls handle the repulsive (yet normal) feelings of wanting to separate from their parent, coupled with a deep desire to still connect. This combination comes out in bantering, wanting to argue every little rule and boundary and sometimes to the point of insulting the parents. The hard truth to swallow for many parents is that this general behavior is normal for the majority of girls. The healthiest (and yet hardest) thing a parent can do is to allow it to happen. This requires the parent to remain calm and avoid being accusatory. It means participating in the bantering and allowing the teenager to express her concerns and points of view. If the parent is feeling defensive and likely to get angry, he or she should end the bantering session and walk away.

**Respecting Their Privacy.** Back to the issue of boys in their rooms; my advice to the mom who asked the question is to NOT force him to leave his door open. That would be a huge mistake, robbing him of his privacy. A parent wanting to take this action is being driven by feelings of fear that the boy may be doing something that must be controlled. Effective parenting means limiting or controlling the nonproductive activities that a teen may be participating in, such as video games, television, or the Internet. Although many adults disagree with me, the teen's bedroom is NOT an acceptable place for cable television, an XBOX, or unfiltered Internet. These entertainment vehicles should be in common area rooms where they can be monitored by the parent.

**Limiting Entertainment Electronics.** As long as a teenager has unlimited access to entertainment electronics, why would he or she want to do anything else? To parents who complain to me that their teens are playing too many video games and not helping out more around the house, I ask, "Why are you not limiting those other activities?" Many tell me that taking them away or limiting them would cause their teen to get angry and explode, and I agree. The emotionally charged outbursts from teens who have things taken away are a result of parenting mistakes made years earlier, such as letting children have cell phones, Facebook accounts, or entertainment electronics in the bedroom. If you have made some of these earlier mistakes, know that you're going to have to face the teenager's fit to realign boundaries that should have been set up much earlier. Don't get angry and fight with them. Admit your mistakes, state the new boundaries clearly, and most important of all, remain calm.

**Re-Establishing Boundaries.** One method for firming up boundaries that may have been lax is the cooperation exercise. It can be used with children ages 6 and up. Set up a time when the child or teen is in a positive mood and more open to learning. Get him to help you build two lists; one of all the things every parent should do (by law) for the child or teen, and another that lists all the privileges that a child or teen has at home. The object of this exercise is to separate rights from the extras that parents don't have to provide, such as entertainment electronics, cell phones, rides to the mall, having friends over, brand name clothing, etc. This creates some important awareness for a child or teen in recognizing the extra things that parents do. Once the privileges are identified, work with your teen at establishing what the boundaries are for each one, such as when, where, and under what conditions. Don't be afraid to stand firm on some boundaries if you feel strong enough. Teenagers will wear a parent down to get as much as they can.

Remember, you can't control what your teenage son does in his room or how long he stays in there, but you can limit and control the things that can create problems. If he's playing too many video games, limit the games. If you're concerned about food rotting in his room, set up parameters about where in the house food can be eaten. If his laundry is piling up, teach him to do his own laundry. And don't let the hormones create fear that will keep you from stepping up and taking charge as an engaged parent. If your son is not submerged in entertainment electronics and lacks motivation to do something outside of his room, then perhaps something else is going on. Some conversation may be necessary to determine if there is something else at play that is keeping him from wanting to participate in a sport or other activities. You'll be more effective as a parent if you preach less and listen more.

# The Care and Feeding of a Tween

On day when my step daughter Olivia was a tween, her mom and I were watching her out the window as she provides us with proof of the characteristics of this age group. The classic tween is an interesting species of the human race, still hanging on to child-like behaviors and yet, demonstrating some signs of maturity. On this day Olivia had two friends over to the house and they were standing by the side of the road, dancing. She was wearing a turquoise colored winter ski cap with a cartoon character on the front, pulled down over her ears, and her female best friend was wearing a brown furry hat, complete with horns, resembling a buffalo head. Standing alongside of the two girls was a mutual male friend from down the street. He wore a comically oversized pair of sunglasses and a bright blue wig from a Dr. Seuss Thing 1 costume. Standing on the sidewalk, they were each doing their own dance routine, attracting the attention of motorists passing by and receiving frequent horn honks of approval. With each blast of a horn, they shouted out with glee over their reward for their comical behavior. While the three of them could have easily passed physically for a young teenager, their behavior indicated otherwise.

**The Power of the Peer.** This sometimes fragile and transitional time for the older child begins a critical phase in development of relationships with peers. In his book *Get Out of My Life, but First Could You Drive Me and Cheryl To the Mall?*, Anthony Wolf, Ph.D. (Farrar, Straus and Giroux Publishing, 2002) tells us that two relationships are most critical to the development of the child; the parent and the peer. But beginning around the age of ten, peers take on a greater role in the tween's and teen's development of their self-image. Their true happiness, he tells us, begins and ends with friends.

**Where Did My Sweet Child Go?** What becomes hard for many parents and other caregivers of tweens is the disconnect they start to feel and observe. The tween begins to take the parent for granted, sees adults in general as flawed and annoying, becomes easily embarrassed by the parents, and, if they do seem to look up to any adults, it is never their own parents. As a result, adults oftentimes feel hurt and angry, feeling the pain of "losing their baby" to the alien that seems to have suddenly inhabited their sweet child's body. The parents become defensive and then accuse their child of being ungrateful for all that the parents have done for them up to this point. However, as experts like Wolf tell us, this disconnect must occur and it must be successful for the evolving child-adult to blossom. The secret is that tweens and teens begin to see themselves as flawed and far from perfect. They then begin to look for the flaws in the adults around them and if they are able to see them in their parents and other adults, they will believe that they too can fit in to their new world. The result will be a successful transition into eventual adulthood. But if the child sees all of the adults as perfect and unblemished, their own self image will be flawed and they will not adapt in a healthy manner.

**Help Your Tween Adapt and Grow.** As I revealed in my own example with Olivia above, we take the measures to provide her with a safe environment within our own home where she can invite her friends to come and "hang out." Immediately following their episode of roadside antics on this one particular day, the three of them retreated to the backyard deck with a stereo, sodas, and a fresh pizza. We were sure to close the glass patio doors to provide them with the feeling of privacy, yet we passed by frequently to check on them. This is the important job of any good parent of tweens and teens, creating the environment that is conducive to social development with peers and yet far enough away from the parents to give them their own space. We set up clear boundaries and check in often.

**Creating Safety for Tweens.** Clear boundaries and limits to the media and electronics that tweens have access to is also critical to creating safety. It is my opinion that too many parents allow their children to have access to dangerous and useless things for three reasons; just because they exist, because everyone else is doing it, or just because they fall victim to their tweens wearing them down. For example, when our child was a tween, all of her friends were asked to turn in their cell phones, PDAs, and laptops while they were with us. We returned the devices to them when it was time for them to go home. It is vital that we know who they are communicating with while in our care. As a result, some of the parents of Olivia's friends were outraged with our decision while others adapted and had their children leave the devices at home. The Internet is no longer the fun and limited novelty that some people think it is. Today if offers unbridled access to things tweens just don't need to see. The increase in cyber bullying has created more danger than good with social media tools such as Facebook and MySpace. Olivia has access to the Internet for any academic purposes that come up in her school work, but entertainment access is limited and controlled. I can't tell you the number of parents who have contacted me for help on this topic. So many of them gave their children unsupervised access to the Internet, a cell phone, or social media tools as tweens or younger, saying back then, "I know my daughter (or son) wouldn't do anything that I wouldn't want her (him) to do." This halo effect in some families creates blindness that is hard to undo when bad things happen.

The tween of today feels more empowered than any generation before them. Without the right frame of mind for the adult caregiver, this empowerment can appear to be mouthy, ungrateful and obnoxious. To be successful with this modern day tween, be open to new ideas and relax. Know that the behavior you see is their way of growing into the strong adolescent you want them to be. It all requires you to give them room, create respectful boundaries, and remain close by to keep them safe.

# How Timeout Should Be Used

Timeout doesn't work as it is used in many families because it is being used as punishment and not as it was originally designed. Timeout should actually be a method for teaching a child how to control him or herself, and should only be used when a child is out of control and NOT for any other situations. When timeout is used as punishment the child does not learn lessons of any value, and instead picks up unhealthy messages that he or she is a bad child and less than whole. Sticking a child in timeout simply serves as a way for the adult to control a child or get even, and gives the caregiver a sense of satisfaction or revenge for what the child did.

**What it Should Be.** Timeout was designed to be used effectively only when a child is out of control and must be removed from a situation so as to regain some self-control and calm down. In this out of control state, some sort of emotional "thunderstorm" has blown in for the child. He may be getting angry and be unable to understand the impacts of his behavior on others around him, nor can he understand any instructions from the caregiver. In this uncontrollable state, he is likely to hurt himself or someone else. By being in the timeout space, the child is given a break from the situation and an opportunity to calm down emotionally. Once he regains some composure, he may be able to return to the activity or previous space.

**Building the Space.** The timeout space should not be a corner or a "naughty chair." Instead, it should be a predetermined space that the adult and child create together. For best results, the timeout space should be a special, reserved spot in the house that will always be there for the child to go to when an emotional outbreak occurs. I even suggest renaming it to avoid the negative connotations associated with the word "timeout." One parent I know used a tiny closet in the house and removed the door. It wasn't convenient for this family to lose the use of this closet, but the need for that space was less important than teaching the child about self-control. Items should be placed in this new space that help use the senses of touch, sight, and sound to soothe the child. A poster with calm, pleasing graphics can be hung and an oversized pillow or a blanket can be placed on the floor. The parent with the tiny closet bought a bean bag chair and placed a small CD player to play gentle, calming music. Allow the child to pick for the space, one special toy or item that the child loves to touch, such as a teddy bear, a koosh ball, or even play dough.

**Getting Them to the Space.** Once the space is created together, the adult must use role play to help the child learn how to associate the overwhelming "stormy" feelings with the process of going to that special place. This role play should be done often and only at times when the child is open to learning and in a positive mood. The adult can even participate in the role play by first playing the role of the child having the fit to help show what the behavior looks like. The mother with the small closet asked her son what it feels like when he gets so angry he wants to hit and throw things. He told her that he "felt growly like a tiger." This helped her put a label on the feeling so she could refer to the role play as "let's play the growly game." Then, when the real moment arrives and the child is overcome with the out-of-control emotion and behaviors, the child should then be guided to that special place in a loving and silent manner. The adult can say, "It looks like you need to go to your special place," but should remain silent after that. In the beginning, the child may have to be carried to the special place. The adult must do so in a completely unconditionally loving manner. If done correctly and consistently by the adult each time, the child will eventually learn to identify the arrival of the emotion and bring himself to the special place. Every child is different and it could take many incidents before the child learns to bring himself to his special place. It's worth mentioning here that the parent with the tiny closet put this into practice consistently over several months of "storms" before she saw results. Then one day when a "storm" hit and her son was about to hit, he stopped himself and screamed, "I'm going to my special place!" He ran down the hall, fell onto his bean bag chair, and fell asleep. The process had finally worked and he brought himself under control.

The message to the child in using this true timeout method is that the child is responsible for bringing himself or herself under control, not anyone else. Think about the opposite message caregivers communicate to children when they act as if to say, "I am responsible for bringing you under control." What inappropriate lessons will the child learn about personal responsibility for behavior as he or she grows older? All we have to do is turn on the news or read a newspaper to see examples of adults with a misguided perception about not being responsible for one's actions.

Two final points that I must make here are the time limit and modeling. First, it is my opinion that a child should NOT be kept in the timeout according to a time limit identified by the adult or by the age of the child. Instead, we should teach our children that they can come out of the special place when they feel they are ready. It is certainly okay for an adult to determine that a child needs more time before coming back to the play area, but the ultimate goal is to teach a child to identify when he can return to the family or classroom situation. This exercise is all about teaching self-control, not control-by-someone-else. The other point is modeling. A parent who wants to successfully teach a child to know when to go to timeout should first have one of her own to model. All too often it is really the parent who needs the timeout, not the child.

# Siblings Sharing Bedrooms

Having two or more siblings sharing a bedroom can be challenging, especially when they are close in age. We may welcome the opportunity for separate rooms, but that is not always possible. I remember wanting to talk and play with my brothers when I shared a bedroom with them. On some nights, I was tired and wanted to go right to sleep, yet one of them would try to keep me awake. Before long, one of our autocratic parents would come running up the stairs with the strap to force us to stop the noise and go to sleep. Thank goodness most modern-day parents don't have a strap (or paddle) in their discipline toolbox. But many parents still yell and get frustrated.

**Remove Distractions.** Getting the kids to settle down and go to sleep means creating an environment that is conducive to sleepiness, which definitely means not having electronics or toys available. All portable game devices should be checked in with the adults before bedtime, and certainly the kids shouldn't use televisions, computers, or video game systems at bedtime. I did allow tabletop CD players for soft music, and some of my children learned to settle down with instrumental tunes.

**Allow Kids to Personalize the Room.** When children can participate in creating something, they are more likely to feel a sense of ownership. With this theory in mind, allow your children to have some say in decorating the bedroom: picking out the comforter for the bed, a special night light, a different lamp shade, or (if you're willing) the color of the paint for the walls. When we were having trouble with getting our two youngest to settle down and stay in their beds, we suggested bed tents to them. They were excited and got to pick out the tent style and couldn't wait to go to bed.

**Together Develop Bedtime Rules.** During daytime hours and well before bedtime, sit down with all the children and allow them to help you come up with the bedtime rules. You can use your family meeting as a time to bring up this discussion item. Avoid overpowering your kids about what the rules WILL be. You'll have more success if you give your children the sense you can't do it without them and need their help. Go around the group and collect ideas about what the rules will be. Offer your ideas, such as staying in their beds and whispering if they have to talk.

**Quiet Time One Hour before Bedtime.** Approximately one hour before bedtime, adopt rules that create quiet time. Anything that could stimulate a child should end, such as electronics, television, and rough or active play. Quiet time can consist of things like getting clothes ready for the next day, picking up toys, and reading. Children learn best through routine and consistency, so create a sequence of traditional bedtime activities in the final 20 minutes before bed. Because you should never assume children will know what to do, it helps to create a checklist or display a string of visual images high on their wall to show the primary steps of bedtime.

**Consequences for Not Settling Down.** Two siblings in the same room may not always settle down at night. If this occurs, avoid getting mad at them and allowing your frustration to get the best of you. Sometimes they are not able to calm down and then feed off of the energy of the other. Also, avoid using punitive consequences that include taking things away from them the next day (a sometimes popular solution). Some small children may have difficulty making the connection and others may just become willing to lose whatever is being removed.

Keeping in mind that effective consequences must be respectful and be related to the problem, one possible solution is to move one of the children. Set up a place in advance. This place should be in a room where no one will be during the evening hours, such as an office, spare room, or the parent's bedroom. Prepare the remote sleep area and let the children know how the process will work. Then, when the children are acting out in their bedroom and you get to the point where you need to intervene, silently enter the room without emotion, and guide or bring one of the children to the secondary sleeping area. The selection process for choosing which child goes should be arbitrary and not based on the incident in any way. You may even want to do it based on the 'luck of the draw' by pulling one of two pre-assigned tokens from a jar, with each token representing one child. It is important to make sure that the alternate sleep area is not set up as being more special than the children's bedroom. This could wreck the plan because it could create incentive for them to want to create bedtime chaos just to sleep in the alternate sleep area.

For best results, children should have their own bedrooms but when that is not possible, try the suggestions outlined above. The caregiver has the power to create an environment that is conducive to sleepiness, but never the power to force a child to sleep.

# Curiosity Killed the Consequence

A mother contacted me for help regarding a recent issue with her 7 year-old son. She told me that he had destroyed the family video camera and as a consequence, she had taken $100 of his birthday money and told him he would have to work off the balance with chores. Mom wanted to know if I thought she had done the right thing. Initially, and without all the details, I gave her credit for not getting angry, not punishing him, and for attempting to use a consequence for a violated agreement or a broken rule. But with mom's next comments, I knew I needed more details about the incident. She told me that no agreements were violated and no rules were broken, and that he just should have known better.

To truly help this mom, I needed more information and at first she seemed apprehensive about revealing what else happened. But there was more to this story, and after hearing it all I changed my opinion. I gave mom some suggestions for backing out of the delivery of the consequence and offered some tips on avoiding this type of problem in the future. What else had happened? Her son dropped the video camera into the bowl while he was videotaping himself using the toilet!

As soon as I heard the story, I knew this was a valuable lesson for many parents. This situation contains so many important components of the very construct of the Love, Limits, & Lessons® methodology. Let me break the components apart and then explain why I no longer supported the consequence as a response to what happened. From the mom's perspective, she was angry that her son was negligent and destroyed a valuable device, and she had every right to feel that way. She felt that he did not use good judgment and care in using the camcorder, and they would now have to either come up with the unexpected cost of replacing it or go without. For a single mom with one income, finding the funds would be no easy task. With great emphasis, she told me that she felt that he should have known better than to use it inappropriately in the first place.

If we look at the situation from the boy's perspective, there are three factors that led him to using the camcorder as he did: 1) seven-year-olds are normally curious about their body, 2) mom did not set up any limits around camcorder use, and 3) just a few days earlier, mom spent some time teaching her son about... digestion. Now we know the rest of the story.

Children are little explorers and are going to be curious; that's how they learn and grow. We certainly can't let their curiosity take them wherever it leads, so we have to do two things: create safe boundaries and agreements to allow them to explore, and keep our emotions in check when they explore a little too far. In the case with this mom, she may have over-reacted emotionally to what happened and may have even gotten angry. Reacting in this way to a child's exploration may discourage them from wanting to explore in the future. And the fact that mom was teaching her son about digestion certainly didn't help and obviously increased his curiosity to explore his body further.

I brought to mom's attention that she had said, "He should have known better not to use it in the bathroom." I acknowledged her for trusting her son with the camcorder and asked her what limits or boundaries she had set up in advance for its use so that he would have known not to use it in the bathroom. She replied, "None." I then told her she should not blame him for taking it into the bathroom because there were no rules set up for camcorder use. She agreed and asked for some suggestions. I also told her we are not always going to have all the rules set-up correctly for every situation, but children learn best when boundaries and limitations are set up in advance. I wasn't expecting her to come up with 180 rules on how and where to use the camcorder. That would be ridiculous. But one simple rule could have been that the camcorder is stored in an "out of his reach" location, and that the son would need to ask permission to use it. In effect, this would be like "signing it out" with either a time limit or an expected return time. Mom could have also used a family meeting to allow her son to help her build a list of appropriate uses of the camcorder along with rules for taking good care of it. Children learn so many life lessons by the examples their parents teach in everyday family living.

Finally, consequences are a good discipline tool but not practical for every situation, such as in this case. In this example, mom had to deal with her son's normal drive of curiosity and exploration. She even "stacked the deck" by teaching him about digestion. She also did not have any rules set up about the camcorder's use. Consequences should only be used when an agreement is violated or rule is broken; neither occurred in this situation. I encouraged mom to tell her son that she changed her mind about the consequences and return the money, and she agreed to spend more time creating boundaries and limits in the future.

# Raising Boys

As I write this chapter, I'm watching a group of high school boys waiting for their bus just across the street from my home office window. It is an early September morning in New England and getting cooler, but still warm enough for an open window. I haven't seen these boys before so they are probably just starting 9th grade. Two of them are arguing and one just hit the other one with his backpack. They are using vulgar language and I'm about to go out and walk across the street to issue them a strong warning. Their bus pulls up. I'll catch them next time.

If my grandfather were here, he might say that the boys were feeling their oats and to leave them alone. This phrase was born in the early 1800's and originally referred to how a horse might kick up and act frisky just after being fed. But this isn't the 1800's and the boys are stepping over a line of appropriate behavior in public. Aside from the fact that they are using cuss words, their inappropriate and loud swearing tells me two possible things about the family they come from: there may be weak or no boundaries at home, or they have poor (or no) role models. These factors are just two of the following seven important requirements for parents raising boys.

**Allow Appropriate Rough-Housing.** I raised two girls and one boy and it was common to see my girls sitting contently, playing together for long periods of time with their tea set or dolls. This is typically how girls engage in learning development. My son however, would bang his trucks together or set up lines of army men to shoot at each other, while making loud explosion noises and occasionally flipping upside down as a way of physically acting out the violence he seemed to be creating with his toys. The hormone testosterone prevalent in males has been linked to aggression. Learning development for boys involves being active and moving about, but that doesn't mean you have to allow them free reign. Rather than allow jumping on the couch, for example, you can create a "jumping" or "tumbling" zone or room for young boys. Respectfully ask rough-housing teenagers to take it outside.

**Communicate with Them Directly.** Two little girls can sit side-by-side, talking away, and hear every word the other is saying, without making eye contact. Because this style of communication is innate in mothers, moms often get frustrated when they issue a command to their son while washing dishes, or shout an order from the next room, and don't get the desired results. Successful communication with boys requires getting to their eye level, speaking in a calm tone, and even placing your hands on their arms or shoulders to make a physical connection. One day my wife said, with her back to me from across the room, "I think we should clean out the closet today." I probably mumbled something like "Uh huh," and walked away. That evening she was disappointed that I didn't clean out the closet, but I hadn't fully registered her comment.

**Teach Them to Express Their Emotions.** Boys who are able to feel their own emotions, and know how to react to them with appropriate behavior, are more likely to be understanding and respectful of others and their feelings. These boys develop a higher level of emotional intelligence and are less likely to be driven by their anger when things don't go their way or when someone makes them mad. They also turn out to be great husbands and fathers. Helping your son feel his emotion requires him to feel comfortable expressing what he feels. To allow this expression, it is important to avoid comments like "big boys don't cry." Whenever you become aware that he is feeling something, either positive or negative, encourage him to express it by asking, "How does that make you feel?" He might think your question sounds weird and may even say something like, "I hate when you ask me that." But ask it anyway. Avoid saying things like, "You shouldn't feel that way," and trying to make everything all better for him.

**Provide Them with Positive Male Role Models.** Boys learn a great deal through what psychologists call observational learning. My grandmother used to call it monkey see, monkey do. A boy learns how to act like a man through the examples set by other men around him. A single mother raising sons needs to find positive role models for them to watch and emulate, such as her father, brothers, or uncles. Women are nurturers by nature. Once a boy reaches the age of eight, he needs less nurturing and more positive male role models as he grows into his adolescent years.

**Institute Firm Boundaries.** As an adjunct instructor in a local community college, I often would have a handful of students at the start of each semester who were not well-disciplined. They would arrive late to class, use their cell phones, put their head down to sleep, or talk with their neighbor. The female offenders usually straightened up their behavior with a quick pep talk, but the males required more convincing. I soon learned that boys needed things presented in black and white and as a result I began including in my syllabus a fully detailed rule sheet with consequences for behavior violations. Boys need clear cut rules that are defined and reinforced. As soon as you relax a rule or boundary, your credibility is shot and they will attempt to bend others. Be firm with them AND respectful.

**Find Ways for Them to be Helpful.** Anthropologists have been educating us for years on the differences between our male and female ancestors. The females remained in caves and huts to nurture the young and feather the nests. The males used their innate aggression to leave the compound to hunt and bring home food. Because of this, males still have internal desires to be self-reliant and achieve accomplishments. Take notice of when your son achieves something and acknowledge him for it. The younger they are, the more you can make a big deal of the achievement. Tweens and adolescents don't often like the public attention, so for them, keep it low-key and subtle. Ask for a brief high-five or give quick thumbs up with a wink.

**Discipline Them Fairly.** Not all challenging behaviors are misbehavior. Some challenging behaviors - such as teasing others, testing boundaries, and exploring - are absolutely normal and merely require some gentle and firm redirection. In my parenting class, while making the point that parents should not overreact or unfairly discipline some behaviors, a man revealed to the class that when he was six- or seven-years-old, he was fascinated with his genitals and liked to play show and tell with this playmates. Whenever his mother caught him, she would end the play session immediately and punish him by yelling, spanking, or banishing him to his room. Eventually she was successful and he stopped. But he shared with us that he was now seeing a therapist to help him deal with the dysfunctional intimacy he had with his wife in his marriage. He said the shame he felt whenever his wife turned down his advances was unbearable. A parent's unnecessary reaction to discovery, exploration, or mistakes by their children can create dysfunction and disorders when they become adults.

Often someone will say to me, "What's the big deal about effective parenting? My parents didn't do any of this stuff you're writing about and I grew up just fine, able to live a somewhat normal life." To them I say, "Why allow your child to have a 'somewhat' normal life when he grows up?" The world is getting more complex, more competitive, and more dysfunctional. Why not take a few extra measures while he is a boy, to help ensure that he will know how to create and maintain powerful relationships when he is man?"

# Teaching Children Manners

Young children do not automatically use good manners. Like apologizing and sharing, learning to use manners is part of a child's social development and is best learned through modeling and coaching, not by force. Young children are very egocentric, meaning they automatically see things from their own perspective and find it difficult to see the world from another's point of view. Because young children have a natural desire to emulate the adults who care for them, these children easily adapt to new habits when they experience good modeling and witness firsthand examples.

Teaching children about manners requires actively taking opportunities to point out good examples on television, in public, or situations created by the caregiver. I remember being with my son at the mall and noticing a man being very kind to his female companion. I stopped my son, got down to his eye level, and discretely pointed out the man's kind behavior. My son acknowledged what he witnessed and we went on with our shopping trip. These teachable moments of proactive parenting carry more weight than any lecturing or scolding.

Your own behavior will teach your child a great deal, so avoid ordering them to "say they're sorry" or getting angry and punishing them when they don't share or say thank you. Be patient as they learn, and acknowledge with excitement when you see your child demonstrate desirable behaviors. I noticed a great example modeling respectful behavior when I was at the playground with my grandchildren. Two small children were being mean to another child – calling him names and intentionally making him feel inadequate. Instead of stepping into the situation and admonishing her children in front of the other child, the mother calmly knelt down to the children's eye level. She told the other child that she was sorry that the kids were being mean to him. She then announced that her children's playtime was over for the day and they could come back and play another day. As she walked away, she calmly told her children that she was disappointed in the way they treated the little boy. She also asked them how they might have felt if someone was treating them the way they treated the other little boy.

Here is a recap on the most important concepts for teaching children manners:

- Avoid demanding, lecturing, or punishing a child into using manners.
- Regularly demonstrate kind behavior.
- To create teachable moments, bring attention to examples around your child .
- Make a big deal when you see them using manners.
- If you see them being unkind, apologize to the victim and end any play or activities.
- Let your child know that you are disappointed in unkind behaviors; do it calmly, at their eye level, and then let it go.

The steps described above can be used for older children as well, except for situations when you see manners demonstrated appropriately. Because not all older children react well to praise or encouragement, it is best to suppress your pleasure and simply offer a low-key "nice job" or thank you to reinforce the positive behavior.

If you have older children who occasionally or suddenly demonstrate poor manners, they may be doing it to "try on" new behaviors as they continue to experiment with their changing and maturing identity. When this occurs, speak to them privately to share your disappointment in the rude behavior and calmly remind them of the behavior that is more appropriate. Avoid drama and keep the coaching moment brief. If you handle the situation this way, they will feel respected and will be more inclined to drop the rude behavior.

Another reason for the sudden change in their behavior could be the need to express anger or revenge for something that occurred earlier. A feeling of being overpowered, not valued, or hurt could cause them to act rudely on purpose. If children know that good manners are important to you, they may be trying to get you to take notice. If this is the case, see if you can determine what may have occurred that would cause them to act out this way. Reconnect with them privately and check in with them to determine if some relationship damage control is necessary.

Whether it's using good manners, following rules, or just cooperating, your child's behavior is communication and offers valuable clues about how they are feeling. Often defiance or a lack of cooperation is an indication that the child feels she has lost her place in the family. Child psychologist Dr. Rudolf Dreikurs wrote in his book, *The Challenge of Parenthood* (1948; Duell, Sloan, Pearce Publishing), "Obstinate children use their behavior as a means of provoking people to fight them. And most parents fall neatly into the trap. Stubbornness is one of the many devices by which children who feel abused or neglected try to attract attention and to demonstrate their strength." If this is the case with your child, go back to developing a relationship before demanding they use manners. They will never willingly be courteous and kind while they are feeling less than respected themselves. Remember, rules without relationship result in rebellion.

# Solutions for Sibling Rivalry

It drives us crazy when our kids fight. What parent doesn't want their children to get along and demonstrate good social skills? But what discipline methods are we suppose to use when arguing, hitting, and fighting break out? As children, we remember what our parents usually did to us when we fought. Most of their disciplinary actions were either counterproductive, unfair, or considered harmful today. Our dilemma is that we know what we DON'T want to do, but we're not really sure what TO do.

Many parents react by first using the timeout technique. The child instigates an argument or fight and the parent sends him to his room, removing the child from the area to think about what he did to cause the problem. Some methodologies even prescribe a time frame for children to be in timeout based on their age. But using timeout rarely achieves the intended goal and simply becomes another ineffective form of punishment. It might stop a behavior temporarily, but it also creates new problems such as undue attention, suppressed anger, and a break down in self-esteem.

The original timeout tool was designed by experts to calmly remove an out-of-control child who is likely to hurt himself or another. The caregiver then sooths the child and allows him to return when he has calmed down completely. The timeout place and the entire process is something that the caregiver should design and practice with the child well in advance so that the child is prepared to experience it and able to adapt. The intention of this form of timeout was that the child will eventually learn to go to a predetermined, special place to calm himself when he senses that the difficult emotions have returned.

Siblings and playmates hit and fight for many reasons and much of it revolves around testing, frustration, imitation, and learning to form relationships. A toddler bites because she hasn't yet developed adequate social skills; a preschooler is unable to express himself in words when he becomes easily frustrated during play; and a school age child strikes another child to test the boundaries or imitate behavior she has seen before.

Putting together a good cake requires a recipe of many ingredients and a multitude of baking actions. Solving behavioral situations with discipline also requires a recipe and cannot be solved with one thing. Here are some suggestions for dealing with hitting and fighting:

• Acknowledge each of the children whenever you catch them getting along. They both need to know what positive behavior looks like. Make a big deal out of it when you see it and thank them for getting along.

• Limit televisions shows or videos that depict inappropriate behavior or poor relationships. Channels such as ABC Family or Nickelodeon masquerade as a children's or family network, yet much of the content sets inappropriate examples.

• Find a time when the children are in good spirits, bring them together, get to their eye level, and explain that hitting is not okay in your family or classroom. Tell them, "Sometimes when people get mad, they need to be alone for a while to calm down." Tell them that from now on, whenever you sense that a fight is likely to occur, you will be separating them to different rooms to play alone for a while. They can also determine on their own when they are ready to come back together to play. Avoid doing this every time you hear an argument and limit it to only when you've absolutely heard enough or when someone's safety is at risk.

• Look for opportunities to teach your children how to express emotion appropriately. Whenever they look like they are frustrated or angry with you, get to their eye level and acknowledge their emotion by saying, "You look like you are really mad at mommy. It's OK to feel mad." Don't say anything more. Don't try to make everything all better or defend yourself when you have laid down a rule or boundary that caused the frustration. You want them to learn that emotions associated with being frustrated are normal and healthy, but controlling our actions is most important.

• When they look like they are angry or frustrated with someone else, do the above plus help them verbalize their feeling by coaching them by saying things like, "It looks like you're mad at your brother because he took your toy. Tell him how it makes you feel when he takes your toy."

• If the fights tend to be over toys that they share, teach the children about the use of a visual timer for taking turns. You should control the timer and set it when they ask.

• Time out as punishment is not okay, but separating them with love and kindness is. If it sounds and looks like things are heating up (not just bantering or bickering) and you've discussed this with them in the past, simply tell them "It looks like the two of you need some alone time" and guide them to separate environments to play or cool down. Use a soft and loving tone of voice and don't say anything more than that. You want to model words and actions that you want them to learn.

• Whenever a tussle begins to erupt, always enter the commotion peacefully, without words, and without emotion. This sets an example of being peaceful and calm and avoids adding to the negative energy. If you're able, love each child at the same time by gently rubbing their backs. This says, "I love you both equally." If they are fighting over an object, ask for the object (don't just take it) by putting your hand out and waiting patiently (without speaking). When they give it to you, thank them for stopping the fight and giving you the object. Tell them that you will return it when they can work together and determine how they will share the object.

• Running in every time there is a tussle or disagreement is also not a good thing to do. It teaches the children that you are responsible for controlling them and they will expect you to do it every time. They may get the message, "I can do whatever I want until mommy controls me." It could even motivate them to do it more often because they will use it to get you involved and engaged whenever they want to feel connected to you, especially if you have been a busy parent.

• It can be difficult watching one child continuously losing his space and being attacked, but it is best to avoid over-protecting one child over another. This could weaken that one child and anger the other. However, if a younger child begins hitting an older sibling, as I stated above, hitting is not okay. The child being hit should be attended to first and allow the hitting child to help you sooth the victim. If this doesn't stop the unwanted behavior, find a way to separate them for a while to play individually. It may not seem fair to the child who did not appear to start the problem, but you can't be sure. No one ever guaranteed that life has to be fair, so avoid making everything fair with your children.

Finally, keep in mind that children don't necessarily see their siblings as loving family members like you do. Instead, they sometimes see them as competition to fight with over toys, space, food, and even mom and dad. They may actually believe that they better get their share of these resources before the other child does. Your role as the parent or teacher is to stay engaged, monitor, set good examples, coach, and not add to the emotion or struggles. You should not make yourself policeman, judge, and jury for every little scuffle. This reaction on your part only reinforces the negative behavior you're trying to stop.

# Ten Tips for the Bedtime Routine

Whether children should be allowed to sleep in bed with their parents or in their own is a personal choice for the adults involved. I can quote experts and present evidence-based data to support both sides of this discussion. This article offers suggestions for those parents who have decided not to practice family bed sharing and who need help in getting the kids to their own beds and remain there.

Bedtime can be a very stressful time of day for families. Parents and children come together after a tiring day of work or school and yearn to reconnect with each other. While parents do want that reconnection, they also see an evening full of tasks that must be attended to before they can truly unwind and relax. But with all those dinner, homework and cleanup tasks that must be accomplished, it becomes difficult to allow that reconnection to occur as it should. Oftentimes, the children feel frustrated, sensing that their caregivers aren't there 100%, so they express the frustration even further through misbehavior and a lack of cooperation.

When bedtime arrives, it can take an hour or more just to get the kids into bed and to remain there. By the time they do, parents are exhausted and dreading having to do it all again tomorrow night. Keep in mind that children don't like to go to bed because it means the end to their day and more importantly, the end to their time with parents. They also seem to have this sense that a party begins once they are put to bed and don't want to miss out, so they will do whatever they can to delay it. To help with this process, here are 10 things parents can do to make bedtime work more effectively.

**Six Preparation Steps for the New Bedtime**
• Allow your child to find some way of personalizing her room. From picking out a new lamp shade to an entirely new paint scheme, letting her be as creative as possible will help her feel as though the room really belongs to her.

• Keep bedtime consistent and on time. Determine what bedtime will be going forward and announce it to the children. If an event or activity causes a late night, don't let the plan fall apart. Reinforce the boundary the following evening and keep moving forward.

• Create a checklist of all bedtime activities that must be completed in the half hour or hour prior to bedtime. Allow them to help you make the list and then post it for all to see. For toddlers and preschoolers, create large drawings or cutouts to represent each activity and tape them at the child's eye level on a wall in sequence.

• Minimize the amount of toys kept in the children's bedroom. They are able to fall asleep best when there are few distractions in their rooms.

• Avoid allowing your children to have entertainment electronics such as televisions, DVD players, computers, or video games in their bedrooms.

• Purchase a visual timer to manage the schedule of bedtime activities.

**Four Steps for Implementing the New Process**
• On the day you decide to begin the new process for bedtime, make an official announcement that you're going to do some different things at bedtime tonight. Be sure to get to the kids eye level and use an exciting tone of voice when announcing the change. Say to them, "Starting tonight, once you're ready for bed and I have tucked you in, I can't speak to or look at you until morning." For younger children, role-play what it will look and feel like. It could frighten them if you suddenly stopped talking. Recreate bedtime with them so they will be prepared with having

you not speaking or looking at them.

• Explain to the children that getting into bed on time and staying there is part of cooperation; the more they cooperate with you, the more likely you are to cooperate with them. Express to them that you are so excited that they are going to cooperate with you.

• Take cooperation one step further by asking for each child's agreement to stay in bed. Ask her to repeat the agreement and then excitedly thank her for cooperating with you.

• Thirty to sixty minutes prior to the official bedtime, announce that getting ready for bedtime has now begun. Bring out the visual timer, set it, and end all stimulating activities, including television and rough play. Make all the bedtime activities, such as brushing teeth, potty, and getting into PJs fun by being playful with them. Children love competition and races, so consider "racing against the clock" with the visual timer to get all the activities completed in time.

Finally, tuck the children into bed with your traditional routines and commit to not using your voice or eye contact until morning. Now here comes the fun part... if they get out of bed, lead them back by placing your hand on their back and guiding them lovingly to their bed without speaking to them or looking at them. Do this as many times as necessary. By doing this, you are communicating to them that you are following through with your original intentions and they will respect you for it all the more. If your child calls out to you and you are sure it is not an emergency, ignore the calls for more water or stories. It is all a tactic to prolong having to go to sleep. If your child becomes uncooperative and collapses on the floor, gently pick him up and bring him to his bed. Do all of this without speaking to him or looking at him, and avoid having any expression on your face. Looks of frustration or anger may delight him and motivate him to keep up the battle. Start this new process on a night when you can stay up a little later, as you may have to make quite a few trips on the first night of this new process. If there are two caregivers in your home, both should be ready to behave the same way and carry out these new procedures.

# Monsters in the Closet –
# Settling Children's Nighttime Fears

When my first child came along and I didn't know any better, I made the fatal "dad mistake" when it came to helping her battle the monsters in her bedroom. Unwittingly, I would frequently grab a baseball bat and head into her room in hopes of quelling her cries for help by standing ready to battle the imaginary monsters. As I lay on the floor swinging at those nonexistent creatures, I remember shouting out in a Ray Romano like voice from the television show Everyone Loves Raymond, "There, I got all those mean monsters and now they are all gone." But, when I got up off the floor and attempted to kiss her goodnight so I could leave, she would announce that the monsters had escaped my attack and were now hiding somewhere else in the room. Each of my next attacks only led to the monsters mysteriously moving to yet another location when finally, my patience would be tried and I would usually end up snapping at her that the monsters were gone and ordering her to "go to sleep." She would end up crying and I would end up feeling badly. I would then try to console her and eventually give in to her pleads of something silly like leaving her light on or letting her stay up later as a means of helping us both feel better.

Based on my conversations with many parents, the scene I described above may be going on in many homes in the evening hours; loving parents trying to solve their children's problems with being frightened at bedtime. Well known pediatrician and expert in child development, T. Berry Brazelton, tells us in his book *Touchpoints* (Perseus Books, 1992) that fear comes in various forms at different stage levels of the child's development. He points out that the occurrence of this fear must happen in order for the child to develop a sense of self-control over the feelings of fear. The onset of fear activates a sudden surge of adrenaline that serves to teach a child how to handle this physiological reaction and to learn to sooth him or herself in that moment. Throughout the various development stages, a child has a number of life experiences that, without warning, throws him or her off balance. These occurrences provide learning opportunities for the child to adjust and adapt to the surrounding world.

Parents unknowingly play a key role in their child's fearful experiences by helping them through it, not making a bigger issue of it than it should be. Without this awareness however, many adults inappropriately set out to eliminate the fear from their child's experience, as I had done, and rob the child of the ability to adapt and self-manage their emotions. It is an uncomfortable situation to see your child hurting emotionally and it becomes an automatic reaction of loving and uninformed parents to want to "make it all better" for their child, rather than allowing them to have the full experience. Caregivers also get in the way of their child's normal emotional development by attaching themselves to an experience their child has that simulates one they themselves have had at a younger age. The child suddenly becomes frightened of dogs. Seeing this reaction in their child, it instantly reignites the unresolved fear of dogs the adult had as a child. The adult then relives this childhood fear, adding their own anxiety to that of the child, inappropriately intensifying the fear for the child.

Giving in to the child and focusing on the monsters is not the answer. I suggest to parents that they help their child focus on what to do about the feeling and not on the monster. I encourage adult caregivers I'm working with to help the child focus on what he or she can do to affect his environment that might be causing the fear. By the time my other two children came along, I had learned not to focus on the monster and instead, helped to coach each of them to determine what they could do that would make their room less scary. In other words, acknowledge the feeling of the fear, but then transfer all of the rest of my energy (and theirs) to helping determine what they could do about it. When my child would say, "There is a monster in my closet (or under the bed)," I would immediately say, "It looks like you're feeling scared... what do you think you could do to make your room less scary?" Sometimes my child would respond with, "I don't know." I would then immediately say, "Make believe you know." This seemed to give them permission to be creative. They would then come up with some possible solutions. One time, the solution my young daughter came up with was "I know; I can sleep with you!" I then said, "That's a good idea, but Daddy is not willing to have anyone else sleep with him... what else can you come up with?" This exercise encouraged her to continue to generate ideas until she thought of one that I was OK with.

Society puts so much emphasis on each of us working so hard to acquire our academic education, but rarely are we taught about the importance of increasing our emotional intelligence. Strangely enough, our prisons are filled with those who can read, write, and add, but it was most likely their inability to manage their emotions that got them there to begin with. The next time your children become fearful about a monster in their closet, simply acknowledge their feelings and then coach them into developing a constructive solution of making their room less scary. The result for them will be feeling like they can adapt, manage their feelings, and realize the power to manipulate their own surroundings to diminish those uncomfortable feelings. It may also lead to you healing unresolved feelings of your own.

# Social Networking Tools Were Intended For Adults, Not Children

It was a call for help from a parent I once helped with parent coaching, about eight years earlier. As she explained how I had helped her immensely in raising her two little girls, who were aged 6 and 8 at the time, it didn't take long to refresh my memory as to how we had crossed paths at one of my earliest parent lectures. Admitting she incorporated most of my advice, she revealed that she was calling for desperate help with one particular issue that she regretted not heeding advice in my teaching - no cell phones or online social networking tools for children.

**What Was Once Cute and Innocent.** This desperate mom explained how she allowed her girls to have cell phones at an early age, pressured by the influence of "everyone else was letting their kids have phones, so what was the big deal." She went on to tell me that it was cute in the beginning when they were little, texting a few of their little friends and getting so excited, sharing information about their latest favorite boy band or outfit they bought. She also liked the fact that she could contact them anytime and anywhere. But things began to change as the girls matured. They grew more secretive about whom they were communicating with and they didn't always answer the phone as quickly as they once did when she called to check on them. And whenever the mom would ask to see the phone, or ask who they were texting, the girls grew more defensive and a casual question began to erupt onto rages that generated screams such as, "You don't trust me," or, "I have a life too ya know!" As the girls became teens, the rages grew so intense that it just became easier for the woman to leave the girls alone and avoid checking up on their cell phone use.

By the end of the call, the woman was in tears and admitted that her now almost 15 year old had been sending inappropriate images to a boy and was setting up a rendezvous outside of the house after the parents had gone to bed. She said to me, "Taking the phones and Internet away is going to be too difficult, so what else do you suggest I do?"

This final statement by this mother is one I have heard many times from parents seeking me out for help. Their child's protective and defensive responses in outbursts of anger have taught the parents to back off and not interfere with the child's unsupervised access to social media tools such as cell phones, email, and Facebook accounts. The parents then find it easier to hope and pray their children will be safe, rather than to take a stand and undo what they started when it was cute and innocent many years earlier. Two astounding statistics came from a survey conducted recently by the online privacy company TRUSTe; that 84% of parents polled actually believe that their children are responsible with private information and 42% of teens polled admitted they will accept Facebook friend requests from people they don't know.

**Do Cell Phones Really Keep Children Safe?** Some parents take the position that they want to be able to contact their children at any time, especially if their child rides a city bus to and from school, or if the parent is ever trapped in a traffic jam or stuck at work. If your child can be found in situations regularly without you or not under the immediate care of an adult, than perhaps a cell phone may be necessary. For these situations, many carriers are now offering devices with parental controls that offer safety and limited use on the device. These features are a good option if the parent is convinced that the child must have a cell phone. It is also important to know that smart children are breaking the security and figuring out how to access the controlled features, or they are getting older and techno-savvy children to do it for them. The bottom line is that setting up a device with parental controls may have good intentions, but it becomes one more thing the parent has to keep track of and control. Feeling overwhelmed with things to remember and police, some end up giving up and removing the limitations just to make life easier for themselves, but dangerous for their children.

Many parents are going to agree with my point of view and have already taken the tough approach to saying no and limiting their child's access to social networking tools. Others are going to read this chapter who have been bitten by the "halo effect" bug in parenting, saying things like, "My child is different, I know she wouldn't do anything I wouldn't want her to do." Some will voice their objections to what I've written here by sending me emails or letters and I will welcome the feedback as a chance for dialogue. To these adults, however, I urge them to consider the effects of the onset of normal changes in their children, like hormones, risk-taking, and curiosity. Consider how these changes will affect the dynamics of what was once cute and innocent when combined with tools intended for adults.

I could have written this chapter solely based on research results and statistics. Instead, I wrote it using evidence I continue to see in my experience working with parents. I once met a mom whose child was a friend of my stepdaughter and who knows many of the other mutual friends of our kids. She revealed to me how she received a friend request from a child who is one of those mutual friends, and accepted the Facebook friend request simply to help keep an eye on her. Not long after becoming online friends, she cautioned this little girl about her language and behavior on Facebook, after reading inappropriate posts. Unfortunately, we both know this little girl's mother is not online herself and falls in the 84% of naïve parents!

One day my stepdaughter's friend shared a shocking fact with me; that a classmate of theirs told them she couldn't live without the next episode of the reality show, *Jersey Shore*! This girl is twelve years old! Liberally thinking parents may be saying, "They are going to see it somewhere, so why be so uptight about it?" Allowing children, tweens, and young teens to watch reality shows like the *Kardashians* and *The Bad Girls*, have a cell phone, and use Facebook, may make them popular parents today, but what are they setting their children and themselves up for when their kids mature?

# Venting Frustration with Your Child

Venting it is healthy, provided it is done in a manner that does not attack the child or harm your relationship with him. You want to avoid saying and doing the things that you'll regret later. The best approach is to express your feelings to your child and then walk away and remain silent until you calm down. The hard part is disciplining yourself to remain quiet and not speak. As a means to practicing this discipline, I recommend an exercise that can be done at home that will help you practice self-control and teach your children how to begin to control themselves as well. It is impossible to do this exercise while at the grocery store, at the park, or at a friend's house, and is simply a means of learning how to manage your frustration in a productive manner.

**A Place to Blow off Steam.** The first step is having a place in the house to go to calm yourself when your temper flairs up. I suggest that the adult identify a room in the house that will be used as the "self-quieting" place to go to cool down. It should have a door that can be locked for privacy. Having things in the room to help you calm down is also a good idea, such as soothing music or guided meditation CDs.

**Creating the Room's Dual Purpose.** Children learn about their world more effectively when things are framed and labeled. Therefore, the dual purpose of this room must be set up, identified, and labeled. Create a simple sign above the doorway to this designated room. It should be one that can be changed or flipped easily to change the identity of the room when needed. A piece of paper or cardstock with the standard name of the room written on one side (such as bedroom or office) and the name of the new purpose (self-quieting or mommy's quiet room) on the other would work well. If your children can't yet read, use pictures.

**Unveiling the New Place.** The next step is to share your new behavior and room with your children. At a time when both you and the kids are in a great mood, call them together, get to their eye level, and admit to them that, "Sometimes mommy gets really mad about things. We all feel this way sometimes and that is OK." You can even help bring them back to a time when they were mad by asking them, "Can anybody remember when you got mad at someone?" You might then say, "Getting mad is OK, but yelling and hitting are not OK. From now on, when mommy is feeling angry, I am going to my special place to calm down and feel better." Take the kids to the door of the designated self-quiet room and demonstrate how this new sign will be changed when you go in the room to calm down.

**Role Play: The Powerful Teacher.** Now it's time to show them what it will look like. Tell the kids that you are going to make believe that you're angry and show them what you will do whenever you get mad. Acting with a little bit of drama, declare to them, "MOMMY IS FEELING MAD! I'M GOING TO MY SPECIAL PLACE TO CALM DOWN!" Immediately, go to your pre-designated room and allow them to follow you. At the door to the room you're about to enter, switch the sign to the side with the word or image of the new use for the room. Go into the room, and close and lock the door. Remain in there for just a few minutes and then emerge with a smile on your face and a look of peace and calmness. Finally, switch the sign back to the word or image that indicates the room is back to normal use, and repeat this exercise a few more times over the next few days. If your children beg to go with you during the role play, allow them to go, but ONLY during the role play. While in the self-quieting room, remain silent and make it appear that you are going through some sort of calming process. If your young child begins to freak out when you go into your self-quieting room during an actual episode of using it, and you're afraid to leave her at that time, allow her to go with you but remain silent while in the room. Children under the age of three are still developing the psychological concept called object permanence, which means that something hidden from their sight still exists. These children sometimes fear that when you enter a room and close the door, you are actually disappearing altogether.

Handling your frustration this way creates a new behavior pattern for you and, at the same time, will help to teach your children that it is OK to get mad and teaches them how to handle it. It begins the process of molding and shaping their emotional intelligence and teaches them that it is up to me to remove myself when I'm angry until I'm able to calm down and feel better. The underlying lesson your children will get is about SELF-CONTROL. Some children may even ask the parent if they, too, can have their own self-quieting space to go to when they feel mad. If they do, help them build one and allow them to role play to teach them how to use it. See the chapter on the proper use of timeout to learn more about setting up a child's self-quieting space.

# What to do When Your Child Misbehaves at School

I am frequently asked for help from parents who have been notified by their child's school that there is a behavior problem with their child in the classroom. The problem can range from a lack of cooperation, to challenging peer interactions, to hitting peers or the teacher. The teacher is frustrated because he or she is running out of solutions. He or she may feel like there is a possibility that the behavior problem could be rooted in something that is going on at home, such as family changes, behavior tolerance, etc., and he or she wants the parent to help resolve it so the child can remain enrolled at the school. On the other hand, the parents are equally frustrated because they may feel like a problem has been dropped in their lap, and that they are powerless to solve it. The parents oftentimes don't see the same behavior issue at home and might feel like it is caused by something in the classroom, such as another child, the teacher, or changes in the classroom setting. Next, the school may issue a warning to the parents, indicating that if the behavior doesn't change soon, the child will not be allowed to continue attending the school or a recommendation will be made to hold the child back one year.

When my oldest daughter was four years old and enrolled in a day care center, her leadership skills began to show early when she began disrupting her classroom group and others by redirecting their activities. Several years later, when she was in first grade, I was notified by her teacher that she was not focusing on her class work and pestering other children around her. In both situations, the school staff was on the verge of giving up. Interestingly enough, twenty-four years later, my daughter was faced with the same predicament when my granddaughter's kindergarten teacher confronted her mother with the same problem.

When parents are first engaged by the teacher in this problem, it can be overwhelming and frustrating. Fearful thoughts begin running through their minds, such as, my child has development issues, she will never have positive relationships, he needs therapy, I can't afford another school, I'll have to quit my job to stay home with her. Some parents may even feel defensive at first and then powerless in stopping a behavior that is outside of the home. It should be assumed that as a professional, the teacher has used all of her classroom discipline tools to diminish the behavior and is turning to the parents as a last resort for help. She may be suggesting that the behavior issue could be rooted in something going on at home and only the parents can fix it.

Through one-on-one parent coaching sessions with parents who contact me on this matter, my first step is to help them determine if this issue could possibly be a learned behavior or a result of family changes. The three most common motives for this challenging behavior are; the child might be acting out to create a result, they are imitating a behavior they have seen, or they are not getting enough rest or nutrition. In the first case, a learned behavior that creates a result is termed by psychologists as operant conditioning; the child has learned that if they behave in a particular way, they can create a result. For example, if the child doesn't cooperate, it makes the teacher raise her voice or the child gets special attention. In the second case, a learned behavior the child saw somewhere is termed by psychologists as observational learning; the child witnesses an interesting behavior demonstrated by someone else and experiments by imitating that same behavior. For example, the child witnesses hitting and imitates it with his peers in the classroom. Finally, a child needs adequate rest and nutrition in his diet. If there are deficiencies in this area of biological needs, the child may get tired at school and act out, be less engaged in the classroom activities, or be less cooperative due to feelings beyond their control.

I encourage the parents to think of any possibilities that could be influencing the child, such as marital issues, parent behavior, influences from other family members, too much entertainment electronics (television, computer or video games), or not enough boundaries and patterns around sleep and eating. If the parent is able to come up with some possible causes, I help them build an action plan to address them immediately. The parent should then share their plan with the teacher to demonstrate they are working on solving the issue.

If the parent is not able to offer any influences away from the classroom, my next step is to help the parent determine if this behavior requires help from a professional, such as a behavior specialist or a therapist. If not, then I feel that the ownership is on the teacher to develop a plan to address this behavior. If the teacher feels that she is unable to solve it using her skills and experience and it is a preschool, then perhaps the child is just not ready for the classroom environment and the parent may have to make other arrangements or find a school with a different environment. Montessori, for example, is not a match for every child and some children act out because they don't have enough language to express their emotions in words. What about the environment - is it too structured for the child or not structured enough? Finally, some students begin to have behavior problems that are really a mask for their struggle with academics. If the child is in an elementary school, the teacher should pull together a team made up of the school psychologist, other pertinent school staff, and the parents to come up with an action plan. Having people with different areas of expertise and various experiences with the child gives a better picture of what will work. Assistant teachers and playground or lunchroom monitors often have noticed things about a child that others don't see.

If you find yourself faced with a similar situation as a parent or a teacher, the first step is to keep an open mind and be ready to brainstorm on possibilities to solve this problem with everyone on the team. Take the time to understand the child's learning style and be sure that the learning structure in the classroom is a good match. Look for professionals who could join the team and provide observation of the child to get a handle on the classroom climate. Many times there are dynamics involved that haven't yet been noticed...moving from center to center before a child is ready, working with a peer who is not a good match, etc. Be ready to come into meetings with an open mind. Getting defensive or being too quick to explain away the behavior will be counterproductive. If classroom or language/learning issues can be ruled out, a different approach might be necessary. Although I generally discourage reward systems, creating motivations works best to help "kick start" appropriate behavior. Younger kids will work hard for stickers, while older students can work for extra computer time or special time with mom or dad. Whatever is motivating for the child and is easy for everyone to be consistent about may be possible solutions. Breaking down the day into a few time periods gives a child a chance to earn rewards and keeps them motivated to try. This also gives the adults a chance to look at the day in separate segments to see if there are consistent problems in one time period or another. In the beginning, only rewards should be used - that way the team can focus on the behavior they do want, not the one you don't. Then over time, the child is asked to show the desired behaviors for longer periods until you can phase out the rewards all together.

# Four Questions to Ask Yourself Before You React

In my work with parents and teachers on solving behavior challenges with children, I help them identify the problem, possible causes of the behavior, and then possible solutions for eliminating it. My goal is to send the adults away with a few simple step-by-step techniques they can implement immediately to bring about quick change at home or in the classroom. To help develop a plan, I play the role of a detective, asking questions that may reveal critical information needed to decipher what is going on. You too can use these questions to help solve your own behavior problems with your children. You may not be able to answer every one of them for every situation, so be patient and do your best to put some thought into each one. Here are four key questions to ask yourself to help you identify a current behavior issue and some common sense solutions to solve them.

### QUESTION # 1: Why can't the behavior occur?
I was standing in the check-out line at a discount store. A man in front of me was in the process of paying for his merchandise while his little girl of about five or six was standing next to him, spinning in place to make her dress twirl. He suddenly reached out and grabbed her by her arm and demanded she stop what she was doing. While waiting in a doctor's waiting room, I observed a young mother as she continuously barked at, threatened, and made numerous demands of her three children to get them to sit still. One was lying beneath the chairs, another one was sorting and resorting the magazines on the table, and the third kept sliding off of her chair as if she were melting.

Adults react unnecessarily when children behave in ways that annoy or embarrass the adult, or add more chaos to their already stressed state of mind. Adults also react in this manner in response to feelings of fear that the child may fall down or get hurt in some fashion. Stop before you react unnecessarily and ask yourself, "What is the worst that could happen if I don't react?," or "Why can't my child do what she's doing at the moment?" Let go of the urge to control everything and everybody. Avoid arranging the outcomes of everyone's behavior.

### QUESTION # 2: How would the child know not to behave this way?

A woman and her boys were walking in front of me at a large mall. They were enjoying some snacks when one of the boys purposely dropped his food wrapper on the ground and kept walking. His mother stopped and demanded that he pick up his trash immediately but the boy would not comply. While visiting friends for dinner, our hostess announced that the food would be served in less than 10 minutes. She then called to her children to shut off the video game and come help prepare the table. When no one arrived, her calling turned to yelling as it took several attempts to get them to cooperate.

Children see the world from a different perspective than adults, and adults unfairly assume or expect children to see it from theirs. Carefully examine the models that your children have around them to learn from and be sure to set good examples that teach what you want them to learn. Encouraging a child to read frequently, for example, works best when they see the adult reading, too. Create agreements ahead of time and set up rules before activities begin, not in the middle of them. Yes, this will require you as a caregiver to think ahead and predict behavior situations that could be challenging.

### QUESTION # 3: What unmet needs might the child be demonstrating?

A parent at one of my workshops shared how her five year old son was drawing and coloring on furniture, the walls, and the floor, and she was at her wits end. Another parent disclosed that the bossiness of her first-born child was getting to be too much for her. My own tween daughter began wearing her hair with her bangs down, covering one eye.

In many instances, both children and adults demonstrate surprising behaviors as a way of getting unmet needs satisfied. The little boy constantly drawing may be exhibiting his need to draw and create. Creating appropriate opportunities for him to draw and color may be all that is necessary to eliminate the problem. Giving a bossy child the opportunity to lead family activities may satisfy his need to be in charge. And relaxing over a tween or teen's experiments with her appearance that doesn't endanger her will satisfy her need to explore her own identity in a healthy way. Have you ever behaved in curious ways to satisfy any unmet needs of your own?

**QUESTION # 4: Is there a purpose to this behavior for the child?**
A little boy continues to pick a fight with his brother. Each time the conflict flairs up, grandma stops her busyness and comes running in to settle the fight. A mother in my parenting class raised concern over the fact that her preschool age daughter had suddenly seemed to regress somewhat, wetting her pants and acting like a baby. This was becoming more annoying now that there was a new baby in the house. When my son was seven or eight, he discovered he was capable of making in incredibly high pitched squeal with this prepubescent voice. Making this noise forced others in the family to respond to him negatively and it became fun for him to get new reactions.

Both children and adults find ways to act out to create more purpose in their life. The little boy picking the fights with his brother discovered that it brought his busy grandmother into the room in hopes of her taking his side. The little girl who had once again become a baby was most likely responding to the jealousy she may have felt of having to share her parents with her new sibling. And my own son found a new way to annoy others by experimenting with sounds he could make with his voice.

Before you get angry and behave badly as a caregiver, step back for one moment, take a deep breath, and ask yourself these four questions. Perhaps the answers they offer may allow you to see the behavior differently and provide you with an opportunity to choose an alternate response that will get you more effective results.

261

Behavior is usually a result of what has been learned through imitation or getting unmet needs or purpose satisfied. Avoid the urge to react and think of ways you can be proactive instead to avoid or eliminate challenging behaviors.

# Parenting Styles and a Little Bit of Dr. Spock

I always welcome feedback to my writing and encourage my readers to write to me to voice their opinion. I've found that the silent majority read my work and take it as encouragement, while others learn tips to enhance the style they've chosen. Occasionally, a few feel strongly enough to write and express how they feel about something they read in my work. With so many different perspectives on discipline in the world of parent education, I don't expect everyone to agree with my point of view. So allow me to take a moment to explain my position on discipline and parenting.

There are two extreme positions or styles of active parenting: autocratic and permissive. Those who support the style of autocratic parenting use high levels of demand and control to manage their child's behavior, and lower levels of warmth and communication. This style is said to be high in control of the child and low in acceptance of the child's feelings or perspective. Parents who choose this style use discipline techniques such as guilt, threats, punishment, and even spanking.

Those who use the permissive style of parenting tend to be more indulgent and offer very few boundaries. These parents give their children too much control and offer very little structure from which their children can learn. This style is said to be low in the need to control the child but high in acceptance of the child's feelings and perspective. Parents who choose this style often find that their children are controlling the relationship.

The autocratic parent may see his child purposely not putting on her shoes as her being defiant and uncooperative. The autocratic parenting model demands that the child put on her shoes now, and is based on the intention of creating a compliant child.

The permissive parent immediately sees his uncooperative child as an expressive spirit and allows her to not have to wear her shoes, or may begin to plead with the child to convince her to put them on.

The third and more desirable style of active parenting is known as authoritative. This style pulls from both extreme styles to create a balance of control and acceptance for the child and the parent. While many parents choose this style today, there is a great deal of confusion and conflict about the balance of control and acceptance, as well as to what degree. The methodology that I teach in my course and materials falls within the authoritative style of parenting, but with a precise amount of control and acceptance. It offers a blend of the positive attributes of the autocratic and permissive styles, but with a high degree of respect for the child and a solid understanding of the child's perspective.

The inspiration for my parenting model came from the published works of psychologists Alfred Adler (1870-1937) and Rudolf Dreikurs (1897-1972), who both taught extensively that a child misbehaves purposely to get his or her needs met in inappropriate ways. Once parents learn to interpret the misbehavior and understand why the child is being uncooperative, they are able help the child get needs met appropriately. As a result, the misbehavior and uncooperativeness stops. Parents actually get more peace and cooperation at home when they learn how to help a child get her needs met appropriately.

I believe that this approach is much healthier than just demanding that a child stop a tantrum or forcing him to comply and cooperate. Because my approach is different for some, I consider my writing and my lectures somewhat of a "parenting buffet:" you take what you like and "try it out," and leave what is uncomfortable or something to try in the future.

Occasionally I hear from readers who say there is absolutely nothing wrong with a swift spank once in a while, and that a child's uncooperativeness needs a stronger response than just a time-out or lecture. These parents are unable to see their child's behavior as communication and demand immediate and unconditional compliance. They also fail to see that discipline is more than just what to do at the moment. There is so much that parents can do to discipline when misbehavior isn't occurring. It is the preventive strategies, thought out in advance, that create cooperation.

Finally, I want to correct some misinformation out there about Dr. Spock. The letters and emails I receive from those who choose to spank sometimes connect the beliefs against spanking with Dr. Spock. One reader wrote, "Dr. Spock wrote extensively about not spanking your child so as not to warp their young minds, and then his own son committed suicide. Perhaps the experts are not always accurate in their assessments." This reader seemed to be saying that because Dr. Spock did not spank his son, his son committed suicide. However, an accurate check of historical records (not the Internet) will reveal that his son did NOT commit suicide. Instead, Dr. Spock's grandson was the one who committed suicide and was diagnosed with schizophrenia. The misinformation was created in 2001 by Ann Graham Lotz during a media interview following the tragedy of 9/11. Once she created this misinformation, it ran wild on the Internet. It is also worth mentioning here (taken directly from numerous academic psychology resources) that psychologist John B. Watson (1878-1958), who is considered by many to be the father of the "tough love" methodology, had two sons. One son attempted suicide unsuccessfully and the other was successful in killing himself in 1963. The surviving son blamed the tragedy on his father's childrearing practices.

# A Child's Challenging Behavior May be a Reflection of Adult Emotional Chaos

I've been working with parents and other caregivers for over fifteen years, helping them find solutions to their children's challenging behaviors. The adults who come to me want to know what to do about the behavior, and providing them with easy-to-apply solutions is my ultimate goal. To get there, I ask the caregivers a series of questions about the behavior and all contributing factors that will help lead me to the underlying problem that is causing the child's challenging behavior. According to leading psychologists, a child's behavior falls into one of these four primary categories: communication, expression of needs, experimentation, or unconscious drives.

**Communications.** When a child is tired, grouchy or whiny, he or she is not likely to walk up to the parent and say, "Gee dad, I'm feeling a little tired right now. Do you mind if I lie down and take a nap?" They are however, very likely to not cooperative, throw a fit, or refuse to get into the car seat. In this case, their behavior is communication about the fact that they have had enough stimulation and need sleep.

**Expression of Needs.** On occasion I would take my 3 year old granddaughter to the mall with me, and, like her mother many years before, I would sometimes end up chasing her through the crowd. In a quick moment, if I let go of her hand, with a mischievous smile she would run from me yelling, "Catch me grandpa!" Her giggling as I captured her told me that she wanted to play with me and her way of expressing that need was to run away and get me to chase after her. This required me to firm up the boundaries on the next trip and to find more appropriate ways to satisfy her need to play.

**Experimentation.** A woman contacted me for help with her five year old. The little girl began walking around on her hands and knees, barking like a dog. She was probably experimenting with the act of pretending to be a dog, to see what it felt like, and to see what the reaction of her adult caregivers would be. The woman initially became very annoyed with the constant barking. Her scolding created a new motivation in her daughter to do it more because it became unexpectedly fun for the little girl to drive mommy crazy!

**Unconscious Drives.** Famed psychodynamic psychologist Sigmund Freud believed that processes are constantly working in the unreachable subconscious region of the mind. These processes are thoughts that can trigger emotions and behaviors in an adult or a child. If a child is living in a situation where adult chaos is present, the chaos can become worry, fear, or anxiety for a child which can then generate challenging behaviors for the caregivers. The adult chaos may be in the form of parents fighting, a single mother feeling and acting stressed, parents or grandparents in conflict, or even a teacher who has not been taking care of herself. Children look to their caregivers for a sense that things are okay and when they don't appear all right, the child is likely to reflect that unstable sense through their own behavior.

Some time ago, a woman sought me out for help with a situation. She told me that her two boys, in the four to seven age range, were fighting each morning at the breakfast table and she couldn't take it anymore. After a few questions about the situation, it became clear to me that she was running around with high energy each morning, trying to get as much housework done that she could; loading the dishwasher, putting in a load of laundry, making lunches, cleaning up, etc. It seemed as if the boys' fighting grew in intensity with their mother's "busy work." During this daily commotion, the woman's communication was also affected, firing constant snipes at the boys to eat, to hurry up, and to stop fighting.

I could feel the stress of this mom's typical morning as she described what took place daily. The boy's adversarial behavior at the breakfast table was most likely a direct reflection of the chaos she was generating at the start of her day and a reflection of being emotionally disconnected from their mother. The only solution I could come up with was a reconnection with the boys before the morning got started. My advice to her was to sit down at the breakfast table with the boys, along with a visual timer set for ten minutes. During that time, she was to speak as little as possible to them with her voice, and in fact, she should avoid speaking all together. I encouraged her to sit silently and to use her face to respond to the things the boys said to her or to each other. I even suggested that she put a piece of painter's tape over her lips if it was going to be difficult for her to refrain from speaking, and to share the purpose of the tape in advance with the boys.

The woman's initial reaction to my advice was not favorable. She thought it was a dumb idea and immediately gave me numerous reasons as to why she didn't have an extra ten minutes available to her each morning. However, because she had no other options and desperately needed a solution, over the next week she implemented my idea and later informed me of the changes in her mornings at home. The fighting between the boys decreased and she actually felt calmer after having the connection time with them.

Examine the challenging behaviors in your children to see if you can link any to emotional chaos that may be going on in your life. Children don't transition well in the morning, when picking them up at the preschool, or when everyone arrives home at the end of the day. Sometimes they just need a connection with their primary caregivers before they can proceed to the next segment of their day. You may find that if you become more peaceful, your children will, too.

# Having the Courage to do it Right

To parent in a way that appears different from the mainstream requires courage and faith that you will make a difference in your child's character. I know the challenge of being true to this courage and faith, because I experienced it as a dad. Many of you are facing the challenge today.

You don't allow your children to be "plugged in" to the video screen without restrictions. You allow your children to express their feelings and have their tantrums. You have limitations on what they can and cannot do or see. You are a parent who has set up respectful rules, agreements, and consequences, and has taken time to develop strong relationships with your children. You are a parent who avoids yelling, punishing, or reacting to your children's testing and who then suffers the wrath of criticism from those who notice when your children test you. You don't provide your young teens with cell phones or allow them to have a MySpace or Facebook page, just because everyone else does. All the while, your family members, parents, neighbors, and even your spouse, may think you've gone overboard and have bought into the "new age" parenting. They may think you are spoiling your child. They judge you, talk behind your back, avoid spending time with you, and even find ways to sabotage what you've created.

Parenting effectively today is difficult for so many reasons. The world is no longer autocratic like the one in which we grew up. There are many differing opinions on how to parent. It is hard to become a parent you've never seen, and the media and advertising culture are not parents' friends. Because we live more complex lives than our parents did, it's often easier just to give in to our children's demands or the pressure of what everyone else is doing.

When I was raising my three children in the 80's and 90's, these difficulties had begun to surface. At times I felt like I was the only one struggling with being a real dad. My father was a poor role model, so I knew what I did not want to be like as a parent. With no support system to help me, making the transition was challenging, but I was committed to doing what I knew was right. Many of my neighbors knew that I was a parent educator but no one ever discussed this topic. My column on discipline ran each month in the local parenting magazine but no one ever acknowledged it. On occasions when I would prevent my children from watching unsuitable movies at a friend's home, or pulled them from a party where inappropriate behavior or activities were going to be allowed, some adults would say to me, "They are going to see it somewhere anyway, so what's the use in making life difficult."

A woman who attended several of my parenting classes revealed how challenging it was to be around judgmental family members who used autocratic parenting methods, such as yelling, threatening, punishing, and scolding. On occasions when she had not taken the time to set up boundaries or agreements in advance with her preschooler, or if he became over tired and hungry at a family gathering, she noticed that her little son became uncooperative. When this happened, she knew that the next step was to simply end the activity and go home. But her family would say that her parenting style was wrong, and instead told her that she should demand that her child behave and comply. After all, she was the parent and should be in charge. She knew in her heart, though, that forcing a child to comply and demanding that a child behave, would only create fear, animosity, and resentfulness in the child. These feelings could then erode the parent/child relationship.

I am writing this chapter for all of you parents who feel like you are alone in the world with your firm AND respectful balanced style of parenting. I encourage you to believe in what you feel is right for your children and to not give up. You must have the faith that what you are doing is right; regardless of what everyone else is doing. You are parenting today to help form and shape your children into the adults you want them to become.

A friend of mine had children who were similar in age to mine and he made it clear that he disagreed with my parenting style. He was a father who loved his children very much and always provided for them. He also used a very permissive style of parenting but would "lose it" regularly and yell and punish. He had no rules or boundaries set up in advance and he let his children pretty much do what they wanted, whether it was watching whatever they wanted on television or buying them whatever they asked for. His children are now in their twenties, have been arrested multiple times, and do not have regular employment or a place to call their own. Did his parenting choices contribute to their bleak disposition? Today, my three children are leading productive lives, keeping themselves safe, building healthy relationships, and following their intuition to find their purpose in this world. Did my choice of parenting style help contribute to their success today as adults? I like to think that it did.

A parent once said to me, "My parents yelled and punished me when I was growing up, and look at me... I have a job, a mortgage, and I'm able to live my life just fine." I replied that I did not want my children to live their life "just fine." I wanted them to live their life to the fullest, to find the work they love, to build awesome relationships, and to find their purpose in this world. Goals like these require parenting differently than everyone else and having the courage to stand alone.

# Help Them Hear the Music Inside

Author Dr. Wayne Dyer once said, "We must not die with our music still inside of us." What I believe he meant by this was that each one of us has very unique and special gifts deep inside — natural skills and talents that we were given. We know that many talents can be acquired and developed with elaborate training, but many others already exist, just waiting to be discovered and honed. Whether it's a flair for the arts and creativity, personal skills such as communication and leadership, or a knack for precision and accuracy, there is something special and unique about each of us. Have you ever noticed how some children have a natural ability to balance and dance, or others who can sing in tune? Years ago, I watched with amazement how a friend's 4-year-old could handle an adult-sized basketball and kick a soccer ball with precision.

To this day, many of us have not yet discovered what unique things we can accomplish just by trying. These gifts are buried too deeply and covered over by our hectic schedules and an inability to reach inside ourselves. I met a grown woman one day who told me about a desire she had always felt to work with or care for animals. She put in long hours in an office and constantly day-dreamed about starting an adoption agency for small pets. I told her that her "calling" will remain a fantasy until she responds to it, and I encouraged her to find ways of exploring possibilities. I met a man several years ago who had a gift for teaching scripture in his church and yet he worked in sales. He eventually answered the "calling" by quitting his job and going to school to become a pastor, something he wished he had done many years earlier.

Some of our inability to live our dream or to love what comes naturally to us stems from the discouragement we experienced as children. Our parents meant well, but often their words and actions hurt our morale and self-image, and caused us to give up. When I was in junior high school, I discovered a passion for reading the works of Edgar Allan Poe and emulating him in my stories and tales. But it seemed that when I showed my work to my parents and teachers, they were quite critical and continued to point out all the things I was doing wrong in my writing. Eventually I became so discouraged that I gave up the love of writing and felt I couldn't live up to their expectations. I know now they all meant well with their comments and criticism. They wanted to help me be the best writer possible, or use a style that they felt would be most effective. But it backfired and caused me to give up. It wasn't until about 10 years ago that I dusted off that internal "calling" to write and began creating work that led me to the publication of this book.

Proverbs 22:6 says, *"Train a child in the way that he should go, and when he is old he will not depart from it."* My interpretation of this passage is that we must not train our children the way we think they should go, but instead the way God intended for them to go. Be sure that you aren't trying to live your dreams through your child. I received the following e-mail from a parent; *"I've seen my daughter draw beautifully but she doesn't seem to care to do it much. Artistic ability runs in our family. How do I encourage our daughter to keep at it so she'll go far?"* Perhaps the parents of this child were putting too much pressure on her to excel at art because they wanted her to be great. The comment about the family's artistic ability may indicate the motivation for the pressure.

I challenge you to see your child as a gift with hidden secrets and treasures within — that only she and the greater powers that created the magic of life itself know her ultimate capabilities. You have the rewarding opportunity to help her unlock these gifts through your encouragement and coaching as a parent. Here are three important things you can do to help her discover what she loves and what she could achieve.

**Allow Your Children to Explore**. Create opportunities for them in all forms of art, creativity, and play. If you see that they have an affinity for something specific, it's fine to encourage them but avoid pressure; otherwise, they may develop an aversion to the activity. Always ask your children their preferences, and help them experience what is most meaningful to them.

**Allow Them to Dream Boldly.** Based on their dreams and desires, allow them to ask for things without criticism. It's important to avoid squelching or discouraging your children's requests based on their creative aspirations. Buy an empty notebook or a colorful essay book so they log their dreams and desires. You don't always have to fulfill their requests. Set an example by joining them and sharing some of your dreams with them.

**Use More Encouragement and Less Praise.** Praise is too judgmental and applies labels to a child. Encouragement empowers kids to listen to their hearts and determine what they think about themselves or what they created. Ask plenty of open-ended questions and allow them to describe to you their opinions and thoughts about something they did or created.

If you've noticed some wonderful artistic ability in your child, cherish it and nourish it. It's desirable to encourage them to excel in that area, but be ready to let go if they choose not to pursue the interest. Don't try to clone yourself in your child, and certainly don't attempt to fulfill your thwarted desires through them. Be your child's coach and guide, and you'll help them find their own unique place in this world. Doing so will help them live a full and happy life, and to hear that song inside them waiting to be sung.

## 10 Things Children Want From Parents

**Please talk less...**
... I need the silence to hear my inner voice so it will guide me.

**Please create rules and boundaries for me and you...**
... I want to learn how to create and keep them for myself.

**Please stop doing too much for me...**
... I need to learn how to do things for myself so I will be capable.

**Please watch what you do...**
... I need you to be a good example for me to learn from.

**Please look real hard...**

... I need you to see me as I really am... just a child.

**Please limit my non-academic computer time and video games...**
... I want to learn how to make time for reading and creative play.

**Please listen closely...**
... I need you to really hear what I have to say.

**Please coach me well...**
... I need you to teach me how to speak up for myself.

**Please treat others with respect...**
... I'm watching you and want to learn how to do the same.

**Please stop buying me everything...**
... Your one-on-one time and attention are far more valuable.

# About the Author

Bill Corbett is a parent educator, professional speaker, and writer on discipline and family matters, and founder and president of Cooperative Kids. As a member of the American Psychological Association and the North American Society for Adlerian Psychology, he provides parent coaching and keynote presentations to parent and professional audiences across the country. Bill is the founder and host of the former radio talk show *PARENT TALK* on the Clear Channel network and the executive producer and host of the public access television show *CREATING COOPERATIVE KIDS*. His practical experience comes as a father of three grown children, a grandfather, and a stepdad to his loving wife Elizabeth's three children.

**Cooperative Kids**

# Workshops & Seminars

Bill Corbett is an award winning trainer and speaker, recognized by Toastmasters International. He has developed and conducted seminars and training sessions for clients such as the states of Connecticut, Tennessee, and Arkansas, and organizations such as National Head Start, and the Association for Education of Young Children (AEYC). Bill was selected as the keynote speaker for the 2005 Child Care Collaborative Conference held at Tennessee Tech University, and his *Love, Limits, & Lessons®* program was featured as the conference title and theme. In 2012, he delivered the keynotes at the Preschool Enrichment Conference in Springfield, MA and the Delaware Valley AEYC conference in Philadelphia, PA.

Here is feedback from a client following one of his sessions:
*"Bill's appreciation for the difficulties of being both a parent AND a child allows him to convey sound advice with compassion, respect, and humor. He taught us that we, as parents, are using antiquated tools to deal with this generation of challenging children. Somehow, Bill encouraged a great deal of audience participation and self-disclosure, without a fear of judgment. We all appreciated his nonjudgmental style and his ability to make us laugh at ourselves!"*
- Lisa Kantor, Co-Chair,     Parent Enrichment Committee
                              Berkshire Country Day School

Call for a customized seminar or keynote for your organization:
   **Cooperative Kids, LLC**
   **info@CooperativeKids.com**
   **www.CooperativeKids.com**

Cooperative Kids

# Become a Trainer...
# ... and Help Change the World

When Bill Corbett began teaching parenting classes and word about his training began to spread, he soon discovered that he couldn't be everywhere. *"I started getting calls from parents in areas I couldn't possibly get to, asking me when I would be teaching a Love, Limits, & Lessons® parenting class in their area. I soon realized that I needed to create a team to help me teach."*

Today Bill trains parents and professionals across the country to teach the parenting class in their local community or within their organization. Those completing the 25 hours of one-on-one training with Bill receive the materials, a certification, and the support to help and train others. Bill says, *"Third-person teaching is the most effective way of developing new skills and parenting is no different. But the ones who will benefit the greatest from your new teaching business will be your own children!"*

Feedback from a certified instructor:
*"I am the CEO of a nonprofit organization that provides parenting classes. We needed an effective program to offer and had the pleasure of spending a long weekend becoming certified in Bill's Love, Limits and Lessons® parenting class. My entire staff and I were wowed! We're all parents as well and we all learned so much about becoming better parents. Bill's passion to teach parents and trainers to raise their kids with love, limits and lessons gave us all a new and powerful view on parenting. We are proud to be a part of his national team."*
- ShawnDella Headley, CEO, Stairway to Hope, NY, New York.

For more information on joining the Cooperative Kids national training team, or bringing an instructor training to your organization, contact us at www.**CooperativeKids.com**.

Cooperative Kids